WHAT CAN BE FOUND IN

JOHN ANKERBERG
DILLON BURROUGHS

D0669081

HARVEST HOUSE PUBLISHERS

EUGENE, OREGON

Unless otherwise indicated, all Scripture quotations are taken from the HOLY BIBLE, NEW INTERNATIONAL VERSION®. NIV®. Copyright©1973, 1978, 1984 by the International Bible Society. Used by permission of Zondervan. All rights reserved.

Verses marked NLT are taken from the *Holy Bible*, New Living Translation, copyright ©1996. Used by permission of Tyndale House Publishers, Inc., Wheaton, IL 60189 USA. All rights reserved.

Verses marked NASB are taken from the New American Standard Bible ®, © 1960, 1962, 1963, 1968, 1971, 1972, 1973, 1975, 1977, 1995 by The Lockman Foundation. Used by permission. (www.Lockman.org)

Verses marked MSG are taken from The Message. Copyright © by Eugene H. Peterson 1993, 1994, 1995, 1996, 2000, 2001, 2002. Used by permission of NavPress Publishing Group.

Verses marked KJV are taken from the King James Version of the Bible.

Verses marked CEV are taken from the Contemporary English Version © 1991, 1992, 1995 by American Bible Society. Used with permission.

Verses marked TLB are taken from *The Living Bible*, Copyright ©1971. Used by permission of Tyndale House Publishers, Inc., Wheaton, IL 60189 USA. All rights reserved.

Italicized text in Scripture quotations indicate author's emphasis.

Cover by Abris, Veneta, Oregon

WHAT CAN BE FOUND IN LOST?
Copyright © 2008 by John Ankerberg and Dillon Burroughs
Published by Harvest House Publishers
Eugene, Oregon 97402
www.harvesthousepublishers.com

Ankerberg, John, 1945-
    What can be found in Lost? / John Ankerberg and Dillon Burroughs.
        p. cm.
    Includes bibliographical references and index.
    ISBN-13: 978-0-7369-2121-3
    ISBN-10: 0-7369-2121-4
    1. Spirituality. 2. Spiritual life—Christianity. 3. Lost (Television program) I. Burroughs, Dillon. II. Title.
BV4501.3.A55 2008
261.5'7—dc22

                                                                              2007034809

Printed in the United States of America
            07 08 09 10 11 12 13 14 15 16 / VP-NI / 10 9 8 7 6 5 4 3 2 1

Contents

"Lost *fans are like Talmudic scholars. They have created a body of scholarship about every episode.*"

—Javier Grillo-Marxuach[1]

Why Should I Read This Book?

> *"What does God have to do to get your attention?"*
> —Rose to Bernard, in "SOS"

I f you're like us, you probably watch a few hours of television each week. If you've opened this book, your television habits probably include an episode of *Lost*'s adrenaline-laced suspense. You're not alone. In its first season, *Lost* averaged 15.5 million viewers per episode. Worldwide, it was the second most-watched show, making *Lost* a global phenomenon. As a popular young adult program, it has also been one of the most downloaded TV shows on iTunes and has been one of ABC's most-viewed online broadcasts. With the explosion of TiVo and DVR technology, *Lost* is also considered "one of the most highly time-shifted shows,"[1] meaning a significant segment of individuals watch the program on their own time outside of its weekly timeslot.

Yr	Timeslot (EDT)	Season Premiere	Season Finale	TV Season	Rank	Viewers (in millions)
1	Wednesday 8:00p	September 22, 2004	May 25, 2005	2004–2005	#14	16.1
2	Wednesday 9:00p	September 21, 2005	May 24, 2006	2005–2006	#14	15.5
3	Wednesday 9:00p (from October 4 to November 8, 2006) Wednesday 10:00p (from February 7, 2007 to May 23, 2007)	October 4, 2006	May 23, 2007	2006–2007	#17	14.6

Source: http://en.wikipedia.org/wiki/Lost_(TV_series)#Fandom_and_popular_culture

Lost has won numerous awards, including the Emmy Award for outstanding drama series in 2005 and best American import at the British Academy Television Awards (also in 2005). You can now find an entire array of *Lost* items, including a video game, board game, magazine, and tie-in novels.[2] The show has become a part of popular culture, being referenced in everything from other television shows to commercials, comic books, and even song lyrics.[3] A sampling of the enormous array of *Lost* merchandise includes:

- jigsaw puzzles
- action figures
- magazine
- audio soundtracks
- video game
- mobile game (for cell phones and other mobile devices)
- iPod game
- board game
- The *Lost* Experience game
- trading cards
- a dharma rubik's cube
- coffee mugs
- clothing (including T-shirts and various hats)

But why should *you* read a book on the spirituality of *Lost?* The answer can be found in Rose's line in the show itself: "What does God have to do to get your attention?" For some, the answer is found through an experience in nature. For others, the answer can be found in religious ritual. But if you are one of the millions of fans of *Lost,* maybe you could experience something about God from a look at the show that you enjoy.

It Sure Doesn't Hurt...

Lost is filmed on location in Hawaii and includes one of the largest casts of any television series today. As a result, it is also one of the most expensive shows in production.[4]

Why do we believe *Lost* has something to teach us regarding faith elements in our lives? A casual viewing of the show reveals that each episode centers on various aspects of life, from which we can learn more about what we believe concerning spiritual issues. For instance, *Lost* regularly discusses…

- the existence of God
- miracles
- the nature of good and evil
- the afterlife
- secrets and lies
- and even baptism, prayer, and the construction of a church!

Wouldn't you like to better understand the ways this show can influence people's thinking? In this book, we'll discuss 13 key issues that highlight important spiritual aspects in our lives today (and you won't even have to push a button!).

Dillon's *Lost* Experiences

Okay, I'll admit it from the start—I'm a *Lost* fanatic. I've watched every episode at least once, analyzed freeze frames of key scenes, contributed to Lostpedia.com, zoomed in on Jack's crossword puzzle and Eko's Jesus Stick for a closer read, and even joined an official academic group focused on *Lost* research. I've even purchased a cast-autographed copy of a *Lost* script on eBay!

Why? Because I really like the show. It keeps people guessing, unlike most other shows on television. More importantly, I enjoy learning how the writers (and viewers) perceive spiritual issues. The more I understand how others (not "the Others") view God and spirituality, the better I can communicate what I believe about Christ in my everyday conversations with people.

Our look at *Lost* will include three parts. First, we'll discuss some of the specific points of dialogue from the first three seasons of *Lost* that touch on various spiritual issues. This will allow us a fuller understanding of what the show itself communicates on these spiritual themes. Second, we'll note what God's Word, the Bible, says about each issue, with an emphasis on both the positive and sometimes cautionary aspects that connect with the show. Finally, we'll end each chapter with some "*Lost* Talk," leaving you with a few discussion questions that can be used in personal or group situations to talk further about what you've learned. Our goal is to provide some suggestions as to how each faith element can be enhanced in your life in practical everyday ways.

Now for our official disclaimer: We're not saying that *Lost* is a Christian show. We only suggest that it addresses the deep spiritual issues people face today. As we take a look at some of the various themes addressed in the show, we hope to help you understand these issues from God's perspective and to live in a way that lines up with the truth of the Bible. We'd also love to hear your thoughts along the way as well. Please feel free to contact us at lost@johnankerberg.org to share your thoughts or questions. We look forward to hearing from you.

Ready to begin? It's time to head to the island…and hear from the words and world of *Lost!*

PART ONE:
The Themes of *Lost*

LOST on God

BEN: *Do you believe in God, Jack?*

JACK: *Do you?*

BEN: *Two days after I found out I had a fatal tumor on my spine, a spinal surgeon fell out of the sky. If that's not proof of God, I don't know what is.*

—FROM "THE COST OF LIVING"

Ben Linus, leader of the Others, who has captured Dr. Jack Shephard during Season Three, asks the unthinkable: for Jack to remove Ben's tumor in order to save his life. Jack's response seems natural from a human perspective when he answers, "All of this... you brought me here to operate on you? You...you want me to save your life?" Yet Ben's response has nothing to do with answering Jack's question. Rather, he appeals to Jack on the basis of faith with a probing question.

"Do you believe in God, Jack?"

This question would come across as awkward in many of today's shows, but is one of many references to God in *Lost*. Why? *Lost* frequently appeals to elements of faith and the supernatural. In doing so, it also appeals to the foundation for all spirituality—addressing the question of belief in God's very existence.

Addressing the Issue: The Biggest Question of All

In recent American surveys, as many as 95 percent of people have professed they believe in God or a higher power—they just can't seem to agree on what that higher power is. In *Lost*, this dominant view is the position taken as well. God's existence is not disputed. Yet defining God is left for the viewer to answer.

Interestingly, throughout the first three seasons of *Lost*, we can observe an insightful trend regarding the use of the word *God* (used 132 times in the first three seasons!). It is either used as slang or in a derogatory fashion, used in reference to a deity, or used regarding an almighty God. The highest number of uses occur in slang (such as "Oh, God!"), but God is often addressed as an almighty being, particularly in the Roman Catholicism of Mr. Eko and his brother Yemi, the Protestant faith of Rose, and the Catholic discussions in the flashbacks of both Charlie and Desmond (a fired monk!). Charlie even calls himself a "rock god."

In their insightful book, *Unlocking the Meaning of* Lost, Lynnette Porter and David Lavery observe:

> Spirituality on the island, as in our outer world, includes many different beliefs, and the expressions of spiritual faith vary as much as the individuals who profess these widely ranging beliefs. *Lost*'s many characters wrestle with their interpretations about what is happening on the island and whether a Divine Creator, a large corporate entity, the Dharma Initiative, the Others, the Monster, or nothing at all is running the show. As is common with any of the series' mysteries, it's left to us—as well as individual characters—to determine which is the "correct" way to interpret scenes and events.[1]

On this issue, *Lost* follows culture. Think about it: In your daily life (not Sunday at church!), how is the term *God* used? Workplace conversations frequently include the word *God* in expressions of anger or excitement, or as a catchall expression similar to "Oh my goodness!" Other times, people talk about God or gods in a general sense. Popular shows even build off this type of usage, such as *American Idol* (*idol* is another word for a god), or winning idols on *Survivor.* We hear about rock gods, swimsuit models are referred to as goddesses, and athletes are sometimes called gods of the diamond or gridiron. People will even usually tolerate discussion of God in a religious sense, so long as it does not invade their own personal beliefs or lifestyles.

Yet for a person to answer the question of God's existence as a *particular kind of God* who requires a change of life or action is often the dividing line. It is perfectly acceptable in our culture to talk *about* God, but it is often considered offensive to ask someone if he or she believes *in* God or to ask personal questions about a person's spiritual life.

At my (Dillon's) high school graduation ceremony, the only way a person could offer a prayer was if he or she were already included in the program as a speaker. One of my friends was co-valedictorian and used part of his speech to offer a graduation prayer. Even in this situation, the exact wording was evaluated by school officials beforehand to make sure the language in the prayer was generic and nonoffensive to the audience. Many city councils have run into this issue, too, as complaints arise when a prayer includes any reference to a particular deity, such as praying in Jesus' name.

God in *Lost*

"And God knows how long we're gonna be here."
—Jack to the island survivors, in "White Rabbit"

"I have little doubt that God has different plans than you being a monk, Desmond. Bigger plans."
—Brother Campbell to Desmond, in "Catch-22"

"God loves you as he loves Jacob."
—on a screen blaring in front of Karl while he is being brainwashed, in "Stranger in a Strange Land"

"You owe God for every life you've taken..."
—Amina to Mr. Eko during a flashback,
in "The Cost of Living"

"Only God knows."
—Mr. Eko, in "The Cost of Living"

What Can Be Found in *Lost*?

Lost often leaves questions about God ultimately unanswered. Instead of Jack responding with a definitive yes or no on his view of deity, he replies with his own question: "Do you?"

Interestingly, Ben, the "bad guy," offers the most definitive answer on the subject. He suggests that coincidence answered his question that God *must* exist. From his perspective, coincidence (a spinal surgeon falling from the sky) equaled purpose (to remove his life-threatening tumor). Purpose led him to respond that there must be a God.

How would you answer the question, Where did everything come from? Philosopher Francis Schaeffer said there are only three basic answers to this question. The first option is that everything came from absolutely nothing. This means that a person is absolutely convinced that the beginning of the universe started from no energy, mass, motion, personality—absolute zero. From nothing came everything. Very few are convinced that this is the case.

The second option is that everything that exists came from an *impersonal* original source. This view suggests that all energy, matter, and other materials developed through a process of randomness and chance. However, if we hold to this view, the logical conclusion is that there is no purpose for our lives. We have no evidence that people are any more valuable than a tree, rock, or drop of water.

Also, recent scientific discoveries are leading many scientists to conclude that this view is unsupportable. Many now suggest that if the universe did have a starting point, then it had to have a starter. If so, this fits with the concept of a creator God, or as scientists define it, a transcendent casual agent.

The third possible option is that everything came from a personal beginning. This is the biblical answer: "In the beginning God created the heavens and the earth" (Genesis 1:1). What is the significance of believing in a personal cause behind the universe? Since people have been personally created by a creator, then we have a purpose for our existence.

In this respect, *Lost* agrees with the biblical perspective. Rather than viewing life as meaningless, *Lost* presents a worldview in which the everyday occurrences of life have a purpose. Purpose, because it is intentional, suggests that someone is orchestrating these intentions. Who? The answer, according to Ben, is God.

The Bible offers two assumptions about God's existence that inform the Christian worldview. First, the Bible begins with the words, "In the beginning God created..." There is no explanation of *whether* there is a God. He is *assumed* as the Creator behind all of creation. Second, the psalmist provided a bottom-line comment on God's existence when he wrote, "The fool says in his heart, 'There is no God'" (Psalm 14:1). Rather than defending God's existence, the Bible presents belief in God as the only reasonable explanation for the universe's complexity and continuation.

In the Bible, God is more than just a Creator; he is a Trinity or Triune. This means that in the nature of the one true God exist three distinct persons—God the Father, God the Son, and God the Spirit. However, it is interesting that *Lost* is very big on God, but not so big on Jesus. In fact, through three seasons, Jesus has been mentioned only nine times—almost always either in a derogatory or a matter-of-fact manner. The one time Jesus is spoken of from a biblical sense is by Eko in connection with baptism. However, even there, his perspective is unorthodox (see the chapter "*Lost* on the Bible").

═══ The Nine References to Jesus in *Lost* ═══

"Backgammon's the oldest game in the world. Archaeologists found sets when they excavated the ruins of ancient Mesopotamia. Five thousand years old. That's older than Jesus Christ."
—LOCKE, IN "PILOT, PART 2"

> "Maybe if you pray every day Jesus Christ will come down from heaven, take two hundred pounds and bring you a decent woman, and a new car. Yes, Jesus can bring you a new car."
> —CARMEN, IN "EVERYBODY HATES HUGO"

> "Oh, that must be Jesus. Hola, momento...Yes, it is Jesus. He wants to know what color car you want."
> —CARMEN, IN "EVERYBODY HATES HUGO"

> "What if I don't? You going to beat me with your Jesus Stick?"
> —CHARLIE, IN "THE 23RD PSALM"

> "It is said that when John the Baptist baptized Jesus the skies opened up and a dove flew down from the sky."
> —EKO, IN "FIRE + WATER" (NOTICE THAT EKO DIDN'T HAVE HIS FACTS QUITE RIGHT—SEE MATTHEW 3:16.)

> "So, you wake up in the middle of the night. You grab your Jesus Stick. You race off into the jungle. You don't call. You don't write?"
> —CHARLIE, IN "THREE MINUTES"

> "Now that's a h— of a Jesus!"
> —DAVID REYES (HURLEY'S DAD), REFERRING TO A GOLD STATUE OF JESUS IN "TRICIA TANAKA IS DEAD"

The Holy Spirit, the third person of the Trinity in Christian beliefs, is also lacking in *Lost*. The word *spirit* is mentioned only four times in *Lost:* 1) "That's the spirit" (Henry in "The Whole Truth" and Kelvin in "Live Together, Die Alone"); 2) Richard's talking about Claire's spirit (attitude) in "Raised by Another"; and 3) in Charlie's reference to Locke's "spirit tent" in "Further Instructions."

There are major differences between believing in *a* god, believing in God, and believing in the God of Christianity. There are some people who believe in *a* god, but not the God of the Bible. Some are Deists, who believe in a Creator God who is uninvolved in our world today. Others believe in one God, but define God *differently* than Christianity. The two major world religions in this category include Judaism and Islam. Judaism believes in the same Creator God as Christians, but does not accept Jesus as God. They, therefore, define God differently. Islam believes in a Creator God named Allah. However, Allah is defined much differently in the Qur'an than the God of the New Testament, especially when it comes to Jesus. In the Qur'an, Jesus is a prophet. In Christianity, Jesus is God (John 1:1).

In biblical Christianity, God the creator entered his creation in the person of Jesus. As Jesus said, "Anyone who has seen me has seen the Father" (John 14:9). Jesus didn't mean we could see the immensity of God by looking at him, but that we could see how God loves, thinks, and acts toward people.

But some ask, "How can we know the information about the God of Christianity is accurate?" For Christians, the answer to this question is found in the historical person of Jesus Christ. Ultimately, the truth about Jesus stands or falls upon the physical resurrection of Jesus from the dead. In our book *What's the Big Deal About Jesus?* we share five historical facts that nearly all scholars, Christian and non-Christian, agree upon about the end of Christ's life. These facts point to the very reasonable conclusion that Jesus did come alive again and that what he said about himself is true. Here are the five facts:

1. The physical death of Jesus on a cross
2. An honorable burial
3. The empty tomb
4. Post-death eyewitness accounts from many people (over 500!)
5. The rapid expansion of early Christianity[2]

Dr. N.T. Wright, the bishop of Durham and former professor at Oxford, arrived at this conclusion based on the evidence:

> In A.D. 20 there's no such a thing as a Christian church. By A.D. 120, the emperor in Rome is getting worried letters from one of his proconsuls in northern Turkey about what

to do about these Christians. So in that one century, you have this extraordinary thing suddenly appearing out of nowhere. All the early Christians for whom we have actual evidence would say, "I'll tell you why it happened. It's because of Jesus of Nazareth and the fact that he was raised from the dead."[3]

If these five facts are true, then there must be some necessary conclusion that accounts for the missing dead body of Jesus and the reports from hundreds of people who claimed to have seen him physically alive after the crucifixion. In addition, those who claimed to have seen him often gave their lives to share this belief with others in faraway places, despite persecution and even death. What is this mysterious X-factor that ignited the birth of Christianity? The option that makes the most sense is that Jesus literally came alive again and proved that he was God.

We find in *Lost* an attitude that is certainly open to God, but often lacking in specifics regarding who God is. Sayid prays to Allah, but he views God much differently from Charlie, a Catholic, or Rose, a Protestant. *Lost* helps to point us toward discussion about God, but the details of that discussion are left to the viewer to sort through.

Lost Talk

- What is your answer to the question, "Do you believe in God?" Upon what evidence is this answer based? What kind of God do you believe in?

- How can what seems like coincidence offer evidence for God's existence?

- In what ways do the Bible's assumptions regarding God seem narrow or intolerant? In what ways do they make sense?

- Why do you think *Lost* mentions God a lot but rarely mentions Jesus? Do you feel this is significant? Why or why not?

LOST on Prayer

JACK: *I've been flying a lot.*

KATE: *What?*

JACK: *Yeah, that golden pass that they gave us. I…I've been using it. Every Friday night I…I fly from LA to Tokyo or Singapore or Sydney…and then I…I get off and I…have a drink and then I fly home.*

KATE: *Why?*

JACK: *Because I want it to crash, Kate. I don't care about anybody else on board. Every little bump we hit or turbulence…I mean I…I actually close my eyes and I pray that I can get back.*

—FROM "THROUGH THE LOOKING GLASS"

The cool-headed, youthful island leader Jack Shephard ends Season Three in a flash-forward scene that offers a mysterious preview of *Lost*'s (possible?) end. In Jack's conversation with Kate, we find Jack's longing to return to the island, even praying for it. In this case, the mention of prayer is intended to show that Jack, a man who has doubts about God, is crying out in desperation to find an answer to his strange dilemma.

Sound familiar? If you're like most Americans, the answer is probably a resounding yes. According to surveys on the prayer habits of Americans, pollster George Barna has observed:

- More than four out of five adults (84%) pray during a typical week.

- Women (89%) are more likely than are men (79%) to pray in a given week.

- Blacks (95%) are more likely than Hispanics (91%), whites (83%), or Asians (51%) to pray in a given week.

- Residents of the South (91%) are the most likely to pray in a typical week. Midwest (87%) and West (78%), Northeast (78%)

- While 98% of born agains pray in a given week, 73% of non-born agains report that they have prayed in the past seven days.[1]

Based on these statistics, at least 70 percent of all Americans pray at least once a week. Why? Again, *Lost* provides several real-life answers.

For instance, in Jack's dialogue with Kate, we learn that his prayers emerge from desperation. In his flash-forward life, he had become dependent on prescription medication, struggled to adjust to his return to "normal" life, wrestled with suicidal thoughts (and a near suicide!), and despised his ongoing loneliness. Each of these issues alone is experienced in the lives of thousands if not millions of people each day. As a result, many of us cry out in frustration over these and numerous other personal problems in prayer.

Another answer can be observed in an intense conversation between Charlie and Locke in "House of the Rising Sun." Here, Locke confronts Charlie about his heroin addiction and reveals, "I know a lot more about pain than you think. I don't envy what you're facing. But I want to help. Do you want your guitar? More than your drug?"

Charlie admits, "More than you know."

Locke answers, "What I know is that this island just might give you what you're looking for, but you have to give the island something."

Charlie asks, "You really think you can find my guitar?"

"Look up, Charlie."

"You're not going to ask me to pray or something?"

"I want you to look up."

Charlie hands over the drugs and then looks up to see his guitar on the side of the mountain.

In this case, Charlie's reference to prayer is sarcastic, but also somewhat sacred. Why? Charlie thinks that Locke is asking him to turn to religion or to God in order to be rescued from his drugs and find his guitar. In a humorous bit of irony, however, "looking up" was a literal looking up to find his guitar hanging above his head.

Charlie finds himself in a discussion about prayer once again later in Season One. Toward the end of "Whatever the Case May Be," Charlie comes at night to Rose, a character portrayed as a praying Christian who struggles with her own issue—believing her husband Bernard is still alive though no one from his section of the plane has been seen since the crash:

CHARLIE: *Your husband was in the tail section of the plane.*

ROSE: *Yes, he was. But he'll be back.*

CHARLIE: *You think he's still alive?*

ROSE: *I know he is.*

CHARLIE: *How?*

ROSE: *I just do. It's a fine line between denial and faith. It's much better on my side.*

CHARLIE: *[Crying] Help me.*

ROSE: *Baby, I'm not the one that can help you. "Heavenly Father, we thank you. We thank you for bringing us together tonight and we ask that you show..."*

While Rose is enduring the same conditions faced by Charlie, she lives with a smile and an attitude of faith. Charlie, desiring this same peace and joy, looks to her for help. Her response was to pray with him in a prayer that fades out as the scene ends.

Addressing the Issue: What is prayer?

There's an old story about a peasant man whose family owed a tremendous debt they could not pay. Unsure of what to do, the man traveled to the castle to ask for the king's assistance. But when he arrived, he had to stand in a winding line with no end in sight. The day ended without him reaching the king, so he returned the next day and the day after that. Finally, discouraged over whether he would ever reach the king, he sat on a stone bench in the king's garden.

A young boy came up to him and asked, "Why are you out here all alone?"

"I came to see the king and ask for his help, but there is a long line. Even if I did reach him, I have no money and no influence to make the king want to help me. I don't know what to do."

"Come with me," the boy said. Curiously, the man followed him to a large guarded gate.

As they arrived, the guards nodded and permitted the boy and the peasant man to enter. They soon arrived at the king's throne room, where the guards backed off and allowed the boy and his new friend direct access to the king. Shocked, the peasant man wondered how a little boy could simply walk up to a place where he had waited for days without success. Then he heard the boy speak.

"Father, this is my new friend. I would like you to hear his request and help him with his situation." The peasant man, shocked, had no idea he had been in the presence of the king's son. However, as a friend to the son, the king mercifully granted the man's request and removed his debt.

In prayer, we often ask for all of our wants and expect God to help. However, the story of the peasant and the king's son is a more accurate picture of what prayer is about. Prayer is the privilege of coming before the one who created us and watches over us, with Jesus as the son who speaks on our behalf.

A famous booklet on prayer gives this simple definition of prayer: "Praying is talking with God." A common dictionary definition is that prayer is "a devout petition to God or an object of worship."[2] However, the Bible provides much more insight into how we as humans connect with God.

The Jewish Scriptures, or the Old Testament, used two specific words to communicate the concept of prayer. The first, *pālal*, occurs 84 different times, and focuses upon the idea of mediation between two groups or individuals, or upon intercession on the behalf of others. The first instance of this word is found in Genesis 20, where, in a dream, God speaks to a king named Abimelech. He commanded Abimelech to return Abraham's wife, Sarah, and said that Abraham would pray for him on his behalf. The text reads, "Now return the man's wife, for he is a prophet, and *he will pray for you* and you will live" (verse 7). Here, the idea is clear that Abraham would specifically pray to God for another person's need.

The second Old Testament word commonly used for prayer is the noun *tepillah*. It appears 77 times and was used in reference both to everyday prayers of individuals as well as official prayers, such as the poetic lyrics found in the Psalms. Interestingly, the Hebrew language made no distinction between official or unofficial prayers based on the different words for prayer.

The original Greek text of the New Testament provides a greater variety of words to describe prayer, four of which can be found in one verse written in a letter from the apostle Paul to Timothy:

> I urge, then, first of all, that *requests, prayers, intercession* and *thanksgiving* be made for everyone—for kings and all those in authority, that we may live peaceful and quiet lives in all godliness and holiness. This is good, and pleases God our Savior, who wants all men to be saved and to come to a knowledge of the truth (1 Timothy 2:1-4).

Each of these words notes a specific aspect of prayer that helps us better understand God's design for prayer. The word translated "requests" is from the Greek word *deēsis*, whose root meaning is "to lack," "be deprived of," or "to be without something." Knowing what is lacking, we plead with God to supply our needs.

The second word, translated "prayers," is a general word for prayer and is used only in reference to God in the Bible. As such, it focuses upon the fact that for Christians, prayer is to be made only to God himself, not to any other deity or person.

A third word, *enteuxis*, is translated here as "intercession" and is used in only one other place in the New Testament. The idea here is that prayer is something we do for others—not only for ourselves or for our own needs or wants. In this particular context, Paul's request is that Christians pray for their government leaders. Why? For the peace of their community and for those who have the opportunity to make known, to leaders, the message of Jesus.

Finally, another New Testament word for prayer is "thanksgiving." This translation is self-explanatory and indicates that prayer is not for giving God a Christmas list, but for taking time to offer gratitude to God for what he has done.

=========== *Lost* on Prayer ===========

"You're not going to ask me to pray or something?"
—Charlie, in "House of the Rising Son"

"Falling down is not exercise. The only time you move is to lift a drumstick from the bucket. Everyday it's the same thing, Hugo...you work, you eat chicken. You have to change your life, Hugo. You think someone else will change it for you? Maybe if you pray every day Jesus Christ will come down from heaven, take two hundred pounds and bring you a decent woman, and a new car. Yes, Jesus can bring you a new car."
—Carmen, in "Everybody Hates Hugo"

"I will pray for her...I will pray for them, too."
—Eko, in "The Other 48 Days"

Rose (to a healer): "So, uh…how does this work? I sit here and you chant or uh…pray, or what?"

—Eko, in "SOS"

"Because I want it to crash, Kate. I don't care about anybody else on board. Every little bump we hit or turbulence…I mean I…I actually close my eyes and I pray that I can get back."

—Jack, in "Through the Looking Glass"

Sayid is also seen offering prayers to Allah on multiple occasions, along with other Muslims, in various flashbacks.

What Can Be Found in *Lost*?

Lost talks much about prayer; and some of it is right on target and in agreement with the Bible's teachings. First, we find our cast of survivors praying for their needs. This certainly fits the biblical concept of lifting up our needs to God, knowing that he cares for us and desires to help us when we call to him (1 Peter 5:7). Second, we find Mr. Eko sharing that he will pray for Bernard's wife and for rescue planes to find them on the island. In the Season Three finale, we even find Charlie crossing himself in prayer as he is about to die in the underwater base.

However, there is a word of caution to be noted regarding prayer in *Lost*. It seems that the characters are able to pray in any way they choose, regardless of who they pray to or how they pray. In biblical Christianity, prayer is to be made only to the Creator God of the Scriptures.

Further, prayer is sometimes spoken of very sarcastically in *Lost*, such as in Carmen's comments to Hugo or in Charlie's remarks to Locke. The ability to communicate with the creator of the universe is not an opportunity to be spoken of negatively. Prayer is rather an amazing privilege—it's an opportunity to thank our Creator and speak to him regarding our needs.

Does God want to answer our prayers? According to the Bible, God responds to prayers with either yes, no, or wait. Though God hears our prayers, he answers each one according to his divine will. As the apostle John said:

> This is the confidence we have in approaching God: that if we ask anything according to his will, he hears us. And if we know that he hears us—whatever we ask—we know that we have what we asked of him (1 John 5:14-15).

The key is to pray according to God's will. What does this mean? God is not obligated to answer our every wish, but only those requests that fit his will for our lives. We can pray for a million dollars, a new Hummer, or to become a professional athlete, but that is not God's plan for most of us. God's ultimate desire is to help us to become more like his son, Jesus. Through prayer we seek to pray God's desires for our lives and thank him as he answers each request. As the philosopher Kierkegaard once observed, "Prayer does not change God, but it changes him who prays."[3]

Lost Talk

- How is praying by yourself different from praying with other people? What are the unique advantages of each type of prayer?

- Why do our prayers often focus on our own personal wants and needs rather than on the concerns of others?

- In what ways do difficult issues in our lives cause us to desire to pray more than usual?

LOST on Destiny

LOCKE: *The island. The island brought us here. This is no ordinary place, you've seen that, I know you have. But the island chose you, too, Jack. It's destiny.*

JACK: *Did you talk with Boone about destiny, John?*

LOCKE: *Boone was a sacrifice the island demanded. What happened to him at that plane was a part of a chain of events that led us here...that led us down a path, that led you and me to this day, to right now.*

JACK: *And where does that path end, John?*

LOCKE: *The path ends at the hatch. The hatch, Jack...all of it...all of it happened so that we could open the hatch.*

JACK: *No, no, we're opening the hatch so that we can survive.*

LOCKE: *Survival is all relative, Jack.*

JACK: *I don't believe in destiny.*

LOCKE: *Yes, you do. You just don't know it yet.*

—FROM "EXODUS, PART THREE"

n the Season One finale, Jack and Locke are working together to open a hatch they have discovered, each with different reasons for doing so. For Jack, it's about survival. For Locke, it's about destiny. This contrast marks part of a much larger contrast between these two characters. Jack longs to return home and get back to normal life as a doctor. Locke's pre-island life, however, was not a place to which he wanted to return. His past included a wheelchair, taking orders at a box company, and a string of frustrating family and personal relationships.

Jack wants to survive. Locke believes the hatch is their destiny.

Which character most resembles your life? Are you just trying to get by and survive, or do you believe your life is driven by destiny?

Addressing the Issue: "It was his destiny."

Lost frequently mentions the intriguing issue of destiny. In the first three seasons, the word *destiny* is used 16 times, and additional references to destiny are implied by the use of the word *purpose* or by claiming an act was something the island demanded. Locke is the character who focuses on destiny the most, with all but two of the references appearing in dialogues that include him.

Why does Locke believe in destiny? An analysis of his character reveals:

1. He has read the stories of other people who have believed in destiny.
2. He has a personal desire to believe in destiny.
3. He believes his ability to walk, after surviving the plane crash, is destiny.

Regardless of one's view about Locke himself, his reasons for believing in destiny aren't too different from the reasons many of us have today. For instance, we often hope our life has an ultimate destiny because of what we have seen in the lives of other people. For instance, as a kid, I (Dillon) was haunted by Obi-Wan Kenobi's words to Luke Skywalker in *Return of the Jedi:* "You cannot escape your destiny. You must face

Darth Vader again." What? He *has* to face Vader? There is no other option? As a child, this statement haunted me.

As adults, we read motivational stories of individuals who have been successful in their personal life or in the business world and wish we could experience the same. Whether your inspiration is Martin Luther King, Jr., Bono, Mother Teresa, Gandhi, or another personality, we often find strength in the stories of those whom we admire, and we desire to implement their traits in our lives.

> *"Don't get mad at me...just because you were dumb enough to fall for the old Wookie prisoner gag."*
> —SAWYER, IN "NOT IN PORTLAND," ONE OF
> MANY STAR WARS REFERENCES IN *LOST*

Just as is the case with Locke, we sometimes find ourselves hoping we have a destiny in life because of negative personal experiences in our past or present. Locke despised his past—he grew up not knowing his parents, was tricked out of one of his kidneys, and felt trapped by his wheelchair and his inability to participate in some things in life. This last facet of Locke's life was highlighted in much detail in a scene in which Locke was forced out of an outback adventure while in Australia. Because he was in a wheelchair, he was told he could not be part of the trip. This experience, among others, markedly influences Locke's actions on the island. Likewise, when we are in trouble financially, between jobs, frustrated with someone close to us, or faced with relationship problems, we seek to make sense of what looks like chaos around us. From this context we seek purpose; we seek a destiny.

Sometimes, like Locke, we also sense destiny in our lives when we experience something we believe is supernatural. In the case of Locke, it was the ability to stand up and walk after the plane crash, despite the fact that he had previously been limited to a wheelchair. I (John) felt a greater sense of purpose for my life after undergoing serious heart bypass surgery and fully recovering in only a few weeks. I (Dillon) certainly sensed God's purpose when my dad bounced back from cancer on two different occasions. When something out of the ordinary occurs in life, we find our explanation not in our own efforts, but in something beyond us—whether we believe it is fate, God, or something else.

Lost on Destiny

"Norman Croucher, double amputee, no legs. He climbed to the top of Mt. Everest. Why? It was his destiny."
—Locke, in "Walkabout"

"That's what you think you've got, old man? Destiny?"
—Randy, in "Walkabout"

"Hey, hey, don't you walk away from me. You don't know who you're dealing with. Don't ever tell me what I can't do, ever. This is destiny. This is destiny. This is…This is my destiny."
—Locke, in "Walkabout"

"What, you think working with your old man is punishment? No, man, this is us taking control of our destiny."
—Michael, in "Special"

"I looked down the barrel of the gun and I believed. I thought it was my destiny to get into this place…And then a light went on. I thought it was a sign. But it wasn't a sign. Probably just you going to the bathroom."
—Locke to Desmond, in "Live Together, Die Alone, Part 2"

"Because you said it's my destiny to turn off that jammer."
—Charlie to Desmond, in "The Looking Glass"

In another interesting situation, Locke turns to the supernatural for guidance by meditating in a sweat tent. During a crisis of faith in the episode "Further Instructions," Locke builds a sweat lodge to purify himself and seek inspiration, yet doesn't know what to expect in return. Locke has a vision and, in a strange role reversal, Boone returns to speak from the dead to provide a clue for Locke's next mission. Boone is portrayed as a forgiving spirit, pushing Locke in his wheelchair. He then leaves Locke to drag his own body up an escalator before receiving his next revelation to find Mr. Eko.

After an odd confrontation with a polar bear, Locke rescues an unconscious Mr. Eko, who reveals Locke's next step—to rescue Jack, Kate, and Sawyer from the Others. This action will bring together Locke's "family" once again. In Locke's case, his destiny is being directed by information provided by the island itself, an interesting mix of religion and action.

What Can Be Found in *Lost*?

On the positive side, *Lost*'s focus on destiny provides an intriguing window into one of the deepest questions of humanity: Why do we exist? This longing for purpose can be found in all human beings in every culture of the world. Among the myriad characters of *Lost*, we find each individual at differing levels of commitment and intensity regarding their own personal destiny and how it influences others.

The first book of the Bible, Genesis, begins with the foundation for humanity's purpose: "In the beginning God created the heavens and the earth." From a Christian perspective, an almighty, Creator God serves as the foundation of our life purpose and destiny.

As the Torah (the first five books of the Bible) later reveals through the life of Moses, the Bible presents destiny as a foundation that is derived *from* God and discovered in obedience *to* God. As the people of Israel traveled and camped in the wilderness in pursuit of the Promised Land, they followed a unique practice: "So they camped or traveled at the Lord's command, and *they did whatever the Lord told them* through Moses" (Numbers 9:23 NLT). The key to their success in their island-like situation was to rely on God's guidance rather than their own insight or the inspiration of others.

This is quite different from what *Lost* and contemporary culture often depict. For instance, Locke seeks his destiny through self-meditation and a vision with Boone's spirit. In our culture, we are often told that we can "achieve what the mind can conceive," or that "the key to success lies within you." On the surface, these catchphrases are attractive because they promote the idea that we can provide our own answers in matters of life. However, God's Word teaches that our wisdom is inadequate and insufficient for dealing with the big questions of life. Only with God's wisdom and the relationship he has provided through Christ can we succeed in finding our true destiny.

Another spiritual principle found in *Lost* is the importance of relationships in influencing our destiny. Locke helps Charlie in his pursuit to give up heroin. Locke helps Eko escape from a polar bear and then, in turn, Eko reveals the next step for Locke's quest. Claire is helped in the birth of her son, Aaron, and later helps provide hope to others through the joy of a young baby during difficult times on the island.

In Christianity, relationships are the center of everything. First, a person's relationship with Christ provides a connection with God's family and serves as the source for all joy. Through friendships, encouragement, and even accountability to others, we are able to encourage one another to live out God's purposes for our lives in a way that is much stronger than attempting to live for God on our own.

Finally, the Bible notes that we find our destiny or purpose in becoming like Christ. The apostle Paul encouraged one group of Christ-followers in this way:

> We keep on praying for you, asking our God to enable you *to live a life worthy of his call.* May he give you the power to accomplish all the good things your faith prompts you to do. Then the name of our Lord Jesus will be honored because of the way you live, and you will be honored along with him. This is all made possible because of the grace of our God and Lord, Jesus Christ (1 Thessalonians 1:11-12 NLT).

In the Bible, destiny is communicated in the word "call." Our destiny as followers of Jesus Christ is to ultimately become more like him in our thoughts and actions. As the apostle Peter encouraged:

> Praise be to the God and Father of our Lord Jesus Christ! In his great mercy he has given us new birth into a living hope through the resurrection of Jesus Christ from the dead, and

into an inheritance that can never perish, spoil or fade—
kept in heaven for you, who through faith are shielded by
God's power (1 Peter 1:3-5).

As we mentioned earlier regarding Francis Schaeffer's three options,
the only option that offers us purpose is the one in which a personal
creator created us. If we have been personally created, we do have a
destiny, both in this world and in the next. And that destiny can be
found as we follow Christ.

Lost Talk

- What are some common ways people attempt to
  discover their destiny?

- In what ways do the relationships we have with
  others determine our destiny?

- How do you feel about the issue of destiny? What
  has caused you to believe this way on the issue?

- Do you believe it is possible to speak about destiny
  apart from talking about God? Why or why not?

LOST on Miracles

DESMOND: *You must have done something worthy of this self-flagellation.*

JACK: *I told her...I made her a promise I couldn't keep...I told her I'd fix her and...I couldn't. I failed.*

DESMOND: *Well, right. Just one thing. What if you did fix her?*

JACK: *I didn't.*

DESMOND: *But what if you did?*

JACK: *You don't know what you're talking about, man.*

DESMOND: *I don't? Why not?*

JACK: *Because with her situation that would be a miracle, brother.*

DESMOND: *Oh...and you don't believe in miracles? Right. Well then, I'm going to give you some advice anyway. You have to lift it up.*

JACK: *Lift it up?*

DESMOND: *Your ankle. You've gotta keep it elevated. It's been nice chatting.*

JACK: *Jack.*

DESMOND: *Jack, I'm Desmond. Well, good luck, brother.
            See you in another life, yeah?*

—FROM "MAN OF SCIENCE, MAN OF FAITH"

There aren't many options available when it comes to what we think about miracles. Either we believe in them, don't believe in them, or don't know if we believe in them. And if we don't know if we believe, it's because miracles happen but we have doubts that they do, or miracles don't happen and we have doubts that they might. Any way we look at them, miracles force us toward a yes or no decision rather than a maybe.

Do you believe in miracles?

Lost presents a series of miracles from its start, beginning with the survival of numerous individuals from a plane crash on a remote island in the South Pacific. From this miraculous beginning the series' twists and turns take us through additional miracle scenarios, both on the island and in flashbacks. These miracles may prompt us to wonder about whether the supernatural is at work in our lives today.

Addressing the Issue: "You don't believe in miracles?"

The episode "Man of Science, Man of Faith" includes the first flashback in which we encounter Desmond, the Scot famous for calling everyone brutha (brother). Here, we find him running stadium steps near Jack, and picking up the pace until Jack's ankle twists. Desmond first asks why Jack was pushing himself so hard, then transitions to a conversation about miracles, saying, "Oh...and you don't believe in miracles? Right. Well then, I'm going to give you some advice anyway. You have to lift it up."

Desmond's words "lift it up" serve a double meaning. While he is speaking of Jack's ankle, the statement also highlights Desmond's viewpoint that there is a higher power at work in this world. But not until much later do we become acquainted with Desmond's belief system, which provides the basis for his advice to Jack.

Lost's focus on the miraculous is extensive. In fact, in our research, we found so many discussions and scenes highlighting the supernatural that it was difficult to put a number to them.

=========== *Lost* **on Miracles** ===========

"Mr. Locke said a miracle happened to him."
—Walt, in "Tabula Rasa"

"Yeah, well, a miracle happened to all of us, Walt. We survived a plane crash. Look, I don't want you hanging around with him anymore."
—Michael to Walt, in "Tabula Rasa"

"I don't know. It's like some miracle. She just showed up with that mixture. She rubbed it on Shannon's chest and ten minutes later she was breathing."
—Boone, in "Confidence Man"

"If by some miracle you manage to get the computer working again you've got to enter the code: 4, 8, 15, 16, 23, 42, hit execute."
—Desmond, in "Orientation"

"Then it's a miracle."
—Jin, speaking about Sun's pregnancy in "The Whole Truth"

"I will report back to my monsignor that there was no miracle here. Your daughter is alive. This is all that matters."
—Mr. Eko, in "?"

"Graybridge come back from two goals down in the final two minutes to win this game! It's a bloody miracle! And right after they win, Jimmy Lennon's going to come through that door and hit the bartender right in the head with a cricket bat because he owes him money!"
—Desmond, explaining one of his flashes, in "Flashes Before Your Eyes"

One particular episode mysteriously titled "?" includes a serious discussion between Eko, a Catholic priest, and Richard Malkin, a psychic, on their reactions to the debated "miracle" regarding Malkin's daughter. Malkin argues that his wife is presenting the situation as a miracle out of spite toward him. When Eko asks why, Malkin answers:

> Because she knows I'm a fraud. Because I make my living
> as a psychic. You see, that's what I do. I gather intelligence
> on people and I exploit it. Every day I meet people looking
> for a miracle. Desperate to find one. But there are none to
> be had. Not in this world anyway.

In an interesting twist, the psychic, who is known for his powers in connection with the supernatural, denies miracles despite evidence to the contrary. To complicate matters even further, Eko answers, "I will report back to my monsignor that there was no miracle here. Your daughter is alive. That is all that matters."

But is that all that matters? What if a miracle *did* take place? Perhaps a supernatural God was attempting to gain the attention of those involved?

A List of *Lost* Miracles

- Locke can walk without a wheelchair after the plane crash in "Pilot."

- Locke miraculously lives after being shot and left for dead in "Through the Looking Glass."

- Rose is cured of terminal cancer after the crash, as shared in "SOS."

- Sun is miraculously pregnant with Jin's child though he is unable to impregnate Sun before the crash onto the island, as revealed in "The Whole Truth."

- Mikhail lives after being pushed through the security fence in "Par Avion."

- Naomi recovers from a near-fatal wound in "Par Avion."

- Mikhail survives a spear shot into his chest in "Through the Looking Glass."
- Ben could walk just days after being paralyzed following his spinal surgery in "The Brig."
- Charlotte returns from death in "?".
- Sarah is able to walk after surgery in "Man of Science, Man of Faith."

What Can Be Found in *Lost*?

Lost presents several instances of miraculous events along with the reactions of those who experience them. But do miracles exist? Many people are curious about miracles, yet are skeptical about them. Because miracles do not fit what we know about life from our everyday experiences, we sometimes doubt whether they can happen at all.

However, facts from psychiatry, medicine, and science are supplying evidence that may indicate miracles are indeed happening in our world today. As I (John) interviewed two researchers about these new findings, I was surprised at the abundance of information that is beginning to show support that miracles do occur.

For example, philosopher and theologian Dr. Gary Habermas said, "I think another factor in favor of the miracles in the New Testament is that there is some very hard data I think that is difficult to explain away. I think of Marcus Borg, who reports recently in one of his books on Jesus that there was a team of psychiatrists who could not explain a couple of possession cases by normal scientific means. I also refer to a double-blind experiment with almost 400 heart patients in San Francisco, in which they were monitored in 26 categories and those who were prayed for were statistically better in 21 out of 26 categories. Because the experiment was performed well, the findings were published in a secular journal, *The Southern Journal of Medicine*.

"So, if you can see some of these things today, maybe you can't say, 'Oh, there's a miracle right there,' but it makes you wonder a little bit. I have to say, can we be so quick to condemn the things Jesus did in the first century?"[1]

Science is also providing more and more evidence that points to the existence of God. If there is scientific evidence that points to the existence of God, then we must be open to the possibility that miracles can happen. Philosopher Dr. William Lane Craig pointed out, "In physics, scientists are quite willing to talk about realities that are quite literally metaphysical in nature—realities that are beyond our space and time dimensions; realities that we cannot directly perceive or know but which we may infer by certain signposts of transcendence in the universe to something beyond it.

"A growing number of scientists now believe that the evidence for the big bang theory points to a simultaneous beginning for all matter, energy, and even the space-time dimensions of the universe. This evidence has led them to place the cause of the universe independent of matter, energy, space, and time. This evidence calls for the strong possibility of the existence of God.

"If there is a creator and designer of the universe who has brought it into being, then clearly he could intervene in the course of history and perform miraculous acts. So in the absence of some sort of a proof of atheism, *it seems to me that we have to be open to the possibility of miracles.*"[2]

> "Unfortunately, we know the experience against miracles to be uniform only if we know that all reports of them are false. And we can know all the reports to be false only if we know already that miracles have never occurred. In fact, we are arguing in a circle."
> —C.S. Lewis, quoted in National Review (April 15, 1988, p. 45)

The miracles that take place in *Lost* often parallel biblical accounts of miracles in terms of how people react to them. For instance, Mr. Eko, a religious leader, doubted the account of a young girl coming back to life from the dead. As a result, he told the girl's father that he would report that no miracle had taken place. Eko's reaction was strikingly similar to the doubts of the Jewish religious leaders who witnessed Jesus' miracles. In fact, Jesus brought a girl back from the dead:

> When he arrived at the house of Jairus, he did not let anyone go in with him except Peter, John and James, and the child's father and mother. Meanwhile, all the people were wailing and mourning for her. "Stop wailing," Jesus said. "She is not dead but asleep." They laughed at him, knowing that she was dead. But he took her by the hand and said, "My child, get up!" Her spirit returned, and at once she stood up. Then Jesus told them to give her something to eat. Her parents were astonished, but he ordered them not to tell anyone what had happened (Luke 8:51-56).

Doubt did not determine whether a miracle had occurred; the truth did. When Eko was faced with the fact the young girl in *Lost* had risen from the dead, he struggled with the conflict between his beliefs and the facts of the investigation. The same was true of many who witnessed the miracles of Jesus. They all saw the same results, but came to different conclusions as to what had happened. In many cases, they could not deny that a miracle had occurred. They could only discredit the source of Jesus' power, claiming it came from Satan rather than God (Matthew 12:24).

The term *miracle* is used in a variety of ways today. For example, sometimes people speak of a miracle sports comeback, as Desmond did regarding Graybridge. Other times, people talk about any act that is out of the ordinary as a miracle, such as Jin's comment that his wife's pregnancy was a miracle. And still other times people use the word *miracle* to describe an event that has no humanly possible explanation—such as the fact Locke could walk after the plane crash when, before, he had been in a wheelchair. In Locke's mind, this could only be defined as a miracle.

Because Locke can now walk, he believes there is some type of special power at work in the island. Though by the end of Season Three he has yet to find all of the answers to his quest, he firmly believes, by faith, not only in miracles, but that miracles happen for a reason.

In the Bible, we see that miracles have purpose. For example, after the Israelites flee Egypt and find their escape route blocked by the Red Sea, God miraculously opens up the sea:

> Moses raised his hand over the sea, and the LORD opened up a path through the water with a strong east wind. The wind blew all that night, turning the seabed into dry land. So the people of Israel walked through the middle of the sea on dry ground, with walls of water on each side! (Exodus 14:21-22 NLT).

The God who created the land and water used his power over these elements in a supernatural way at just the time his people needed it most. Miracles are one of God's ways of showing that he is God.

When Jesus performed his first miracle, it was with a specific purpose. Many who read the account of Jesus turning water into wine at a wedding focus their attention on the nature of the wine itself. However, the miracle was for a much more significant purpose. The end of the section tells us that, "This act in Cana of Galilee was the first sign Jesus gave, the first glimpse of his glory. And *his disciples believed in him*" (John 2:11 MSG).

SOME WELL-KNOWN MIRACLES BY JESUS[3]

Miracle	Scripture Passage
Turns water into wine	John 2:1-11
Orders the wind and waves to be quiet	Mark 4:35-41
Walks on water	Matthew 14:22-33
With five loaves and two fishes, feeds a crowd of about 5000 people	Matthew 14:13-21
Raises Lazarus to life	John 11:17-44
Raises a dead girl to life	Matthew 9:18-26
Gives sight to a man born blind	John 9:1-41

Cures the woman who had been bleeding for 12 years	Matthew 9:20-22
Cures a man of evil spirits	Mark 5:1-20
Heals ten men with leprosy	Luke 17:11-19
Heals a crippled man	Mark 2:1-12
Heals a man who was deaf and could hardly talk	Mark 7:31-37
Heals the high priest's servant after the man's ear is cut off	Luke 22:49-51

Ultimately, God provides miracles to draw us closer to him or increase our commitment. The miracles of Jesus caused his followers to believe in him. Still today, when we see an activity that does not fit our reference of human understanding, perhaps it is God seeking to draw our hearts toward him.

Lost Talk

- Do you think miracles happen today? Why or why not?

- If someone claimed to have just experienced a miracle, what information would you need as proof that the person was telling the truth?

- In what ways do miracles provide evidence that God exists? How did Jesus' miracles help prove he was God's Son?

LOST on Trust and Secrets

HENRY: *Wow, you guys have some real trust issues, don't you? Guess it makes sense she didn't tell you. I mean, with the two of you fighting all the time. Of course, if I was one of them, these people that you seem to think are your enemies, what would I do? Well, there'd be no balloon, so I'd draw a map to a real secluded place like a cave or some underbrush...good place for a trap...an ambush. And when your friends got there a bunch of my people would be waiting for them. Then they'd use them to trade for me. I guess it's a good thing I'm not one of them, huh? You guys got any milk?*

—HENRY (BEN LINUS) TO LOCKE
AND JACK, IN "THE WHOLE TRUTH"

This is one of my (Dillon's) favorite quotes from *Lost*—in which Henry turns the question of trust into a psychological mind game for Jack and Locke. Instead of letting his captivity shut him down, Henry created confusion and distrust among his captors to help in his escape.

When you think about it, distrust or secrecy has caused many of the problems for the survivors of Oceanic's Flight 815. For example:

- The initial fight between Sawyer and Sayid, in which Sawyer accused Sayid of being a terrorist.
- Sawyer being tortured for inhalers he didn't have.
- The fight between Jin and Michael over the watch.
- Jin's detainment for the burning of the raft (even though it was Walt!).
- Walt, Sawyer, and Jin thrown into a pit by Ana-Lucia and Eko for being Others.
- Nathan being thrown in the pit by Ana-Lucia.
- Shannon trying to kill Locke over Boone's death.
- Shannon's accidental death when the two groups met.[1]

And these are from just the first two seasons! In fact, it is those same situations that drove the plot in those episodes, causing viewers to wonder what would happen next. The use of plots in which secrecy plays a key role helps keep viewers engaged because they have a longing to understand the truth behind the secrets.

Addressing the Issue: "We've got trust issues."

Libby, one of the characters from the tail section of the plane, stated it best when she told Michael, "We've got trust issues." Why? Because for the tail section group, several of their fellow survivors have disappeared, a mole had infiltrated their numbers, and multiple deaths had already taken place. When Jin, Michael, and Sawyer's raft landed on the beach and they were discovered by the other survivors, they were not welcomed, but rather thrown into a pit until their story could be proven true. Why the harsh treatment? There had already been too many secrets. Or, as Libby put it, they had trust issues.

In Season Three, we find that secrets become important once again as Juliet suggests that Jack should let Ben die during surgery while she is seemingly posing as one of the Others. When the truth comes out in the operating room, tempers flare and decisions must be made quickly regarding whose side Juliet is really on.

=========== **Secret Stuff** ===========

CHARLIE: *Anyone want to venture a guess as to what Jack's going to be showing us out here in the middle of nowhere?*

HURLEY: *I don't know...stuff. Probably secret stuff.*

CHARLIE: *Why does everything have to be such a secret? How about some openness for a change?*

—FROM "GREATEST HITS"

Of all the characters, it is the chief bad guy, Ben Linus, who plays the secrecy game the best. When introduced, he claims to have landed on the island in a hot air balloon. When the truth is discovered, it is too late to do anything about it because Ben has already escaped through the efforts of Michael, a survivor serving the Others to win back his son Walt. Later we find Jack, Kate, and Sawyer in captivity with the Others, and the Others are claiming to be the good guys. Not only are good and evil a question mark at the time, but the issue of truth and secrets dominates the dialogue every step of the way. As lostpedia.com notes:

> Whether it's to cover deep-seated Daddy issues, or more insidious motives, nearly every character on *Lost* has engaged in some type of deception. These lies (and in the more elaborate cases "cons") have become an integral part of the mystery of the show.[2]

The word *trust* is uttered frequently on *Lost*. It was used 82 times during the first three seasons. Season Three includes nearly half of the occurrences, with 40 uses of the word. *Secret* is also used extensively— nearly 30 times in the series.

========= *Lost* on…Trust: =========

"Don't trust her. She's dangerous."
—EDWARD, IN "TABULA RASA"

"Why don't you trust me, Sayid?"
—LOCKE TO SAYID, IN "THE GREATER GOOD"

"Great plan, Moonbeam. And after that we can sing Kumbaya and do trust falls."
—SAWYER, IN "NUMBERS"

========= *Lost* on…Secrets: =========

"Walt, do you want to know a secret?"
—LOCKE, IN "PILOT, PART 2"

"Don't worry puddin', your secret's safe with me."
—SAWYER TO KATE, IN "BORN TO RUN"

"Can I tell you a secret?"
—JIN TO SUN, IN "…AND FOUND"

"Well, well, lookie who's got a secret stash?"
—SAWYER, IN "ONE OF THEM"

"Michael cannot sense we know he is lying. All we have is the element of surprise, Jack. Right now it's only your responsibility to keep it secret."
—SAYID, IN "LIVE TOGETHER, DIE ALONE, PART 1"

"So now you know our secret. How about you tell us yours?"
—LOCKE, IN "TRICIA TANAKA IS DEAD"

"Can you keep a secret?"
—HURLEY, IN "THE BRIG"

"Why does everything have to be such a secret? How about some openness for a change?"
—CHARLIE, IN "GREATEST HITS"

"We kept the parachute lady secret."
—Hurley, in "Greatest Hits"

What Can Be Found in *Lost*?

Lost reveals that secrets and lies can hurt us emotionally and ruin relationships with friends and those whom we love. Truth is important. Jesus taught that he was the way, the truth, and the life (John 14:6). In other words, he not only claimed to teach truth but to *be* the truth. Second, Jesus promised that those who believed his teachings would "know the truth, and the truth [about life, God, eternity, salvation, and personal identity] will set you free" (John 8:32).

How does this correspond with how trust and secrets are presented on *Lost?* On the positive side, *Lost* presents a variety of individuals seeking the truth about the various issues facing their own lives. This is to be expected because God has hardwired us to seek truth. Claire wants to know the truth about whether her baby is okay. Jack wants to know the truth about Kate's past. Hurley wants to tell the truth about winning the lottery, though no one will believe him. In these and many other situations, the characters desire to know or speak the truth of their situations.

On the flip side, God has always spoken strongly against lying. The prophet Samuel condemned the first Israelite king, Saul, for lying to him (1 Samuel 15:13-34). A couple in the early church dropped dead when they lied about the money they gave to the apostles (Acts 5:1-11). The act of telling a lie can destroy our integrity in our relationships with God and those around us.

In addition, lies can lead to further problems. For example, Sawyer's lies regarding his hidden stash of medical supplies led to his torture by Sayid. Lies by Kate about her past led to further problems until she was finally arrested for her crimes. The apostle Paul wrote, "Stop telling lies. Let us tell our neighbors the truth" (Ephesians 4:25 TLB).

Though keeping a secret may sometimes be important, telling the truth is of utmost importance. When we lie to friends and other loved ones, we cause pain and distrust in our relationships. Even if we mean to protect or help the other person, the end result is similar to what *Lost* presents in its episodes—conflict and trust issues.

But how does this apply to growing in a relationship with God? A story from long ago may share this best. The king of a great nation once noticed an attractive female and invited her to stay with him for an evening, even though she was already married. The invitation soon turned into a night of adultery. The woman later secretly reported to the king that she had become pregnant during their time together. In order to cover up this potentially embarrassing political scenario, the king recalled the woman's husband from military duty so the couple could spend time together. The king hoped that the husband would then assume the baby was his. The plan backfired, so the king took a desperate measure. Contacting the man's military commander discreetly, he issued a memo that commanded that this husband's unit be deployed in the fiercest area of battle.

Later it was reported to the king that substantial loss of life had taken place during this battle, and that the husband had died during the conflict. The king later married the widowed pregnant woman and continued on as if nothing had happened.

Unfortunately, the secret was leaked and the king was confronted by a trusted member of his cabinet. The king confessed the scandal, and his legacy was never quite the same.

The king in this story was David, the man many of us know as the little David who killed Goliath and later became king of Israel. Though he was considered a man after God's heart, his lies and cover-up resulted in a legacy that hurt his own life, the lives of his family, and marked his nation (see 2 Samuel 11–12).

Fortunately, when David was confronted about his lies, he chose to confess rather than cover up. While his confession did not remove the consequences of his lies, it did provide freedom from guilt and hope to carry on. We find some of this attitude shared in Psalm 51, where David wrote,

Purify me from my sins, and I will be clean; wash me, and I will be whiter than snow. Oh, give me back my joy again; you have broken me—now let me rejoice. Don't keep looking at my sins. Remove the stain of my guilt. Create in me a clean heart, O God. Renew a loyal spirit within me (51:7-10 NLT).

Many people assume they could never come to God because their life is too messed up. David's example shows what God truly wants. He desires us to come to him and confess that we are messed up so he can begin the work of changing our lives.

Pastor Erwin Lutzer shared a perfect picture of this in an interview I (John) did with him. He said to imagine there are two roads. The first path has a couple of bumps, but is otherwise smooth for travel. The second road includes numerous rough places, including potholes large enough to damage your car. During a winter storm, two feet of snow falls on these two roads. Which one is better now? They're both the same. Every flaw has been filled in and covered with white.

Beginning a relationship with Jesus is much like these two paths. Ultimately, it doesn't matter what our life looks like when we come to him. What matters is that when we approach Jesus, his forgiveness is able to cover all our rough spots and offer us a fresh start. No matter what past secrets or lies we have told, God's cleansing offers us the opportunity to begin again.

Lost Talk

- Do you feel it is sometimes important to keep secrets? Why or why not?

- Why is trust so vital to a healthy relationship? In what ways does distrust hurt a relationship?

- Do you believe it is ever acceptable to lie to help another person who might be in harm? What is your basis for this belief?

LOST on Good and Evil

EKO: *I'm going to make this easy for you. You will make us priests, and we will fly the drugs out ourselves.*

YEMI: *Make you priests?*

EKO: *Just sign these ordination documents, and I will give you the money for the vaccines.*

YEMI: *Leave this church now, Eko. Go. Now.*

EKO: *Yemi, I understand that you live in a world where righteousness and evil seem very far apart, but that is not the real world. I am your brother and I would never do anything to hurt you, but my friends…if you do not do what I ask…they will burn this church to the ground. Is that worth less than the price of your name on a piece of paper? Think of the lives you will save.*

(After a mental struggle, Yemi grabs the papers and signs them.)

—FROM "THE 23RD PSALM"

Eko and Yemi are two brothers from a small town in Nigeria. Eko is taken in by drug lords who train him as a protector and fellow worker. We find Yemi at the opposite extreme as an adult, a man who serves as the local Catholic priest for his community. Eko, with a desire to help others while still serving his employer, suggests a plan he considers a win-win operation. Yemi makes Eko and his associates priests so they can smuggle drugs out of the country inside statues of the Virgin Mary, and Yemi, in turn, receives money he can use to buy vaccines that can help save the lives of his people.

The key turning point in the dialogue comes from Eko, who comments, "Yemi, I understand that you live in a world where righteousness and evil seem very far apart, but that is not the real world." Are good and evil concepts that are black and white and clearly defined? Or is that an unrealistic perspective? Was Eko right to do wrong in order to help others in need, or was Yemi right to argue and take a stand based on principles?

Addressing the Issue: "A world where righteousness and evil seem very far apart."

Lost presents a world full of vivid examples of both extreme good and extreme evil in action. The castaways work together to help those in danger at the plane crash site and help one another to find food and water and to build shelter. Yet characters are often involved in evil, even among the survivors. Sawyer steals from dead bodies and hoards resources to himself (including pornographic magazines), Charlie drags Sun into the jungle with a hood over her head, Walt burns the first raft, Sayid tortures Sawyer, and Michael betrays his friends to win back his son and escape the island. And these are just the good guys!

The Others call themselves the good guys, but imprison numerous survivors (especially Sawyer, Kate, and Jack), brainwash Karl, and kidnap children who survived the crash. Yet even this odd tribe lets Michael and Walt leave the island, extends kindness to Kate when she is first captured, and allows Locke to join their group.

This contrast of good and evil in both the good and bad guys has been analyzed by many in the *Lost* fan world. For instance, just a brief look at the use of black and white reveals:

- While playing backgammon in "Pilot, Part 2," Locke holds up the backgammon pieces for Walt and states, "Two players, two sides, one is light, one is dark."

- The two stones found on the bodies in the cave are black and white.

- When Claire has her nightmares, Locke has one white eye and one black eye.

- The glasses made for Sawyer are a fusing of two frames: one white and one black.

- Charlie's shoes, in which he hid his drugs, had a black-and-white checkerboard pattern.

- Inside the Swan station is a handpainted wall that has a large black face and a large white face on it.

- Bernard used black rocks on a white beach to make an SOS sign.

- The Dharma Initiative logo has black graphics over a white background.[1]

Earlier in the series, there were points at which the audience was left guessing whether the Others really were the good guys or not. Though it is later revealed that the Others are out to harm the survivors (for certain), there are at least some Others who are not fully committed to the operation.

Juliet completely leaves the Others by late in Season Three. During Jack's captivity, we find Juliet suggesting that Jack let Ben die during his operation. When Kate and Sawyer flee the Others' complex, it is Juliet who shoots one of her own people to allow them to escape. Later, she is sent with Jack to spy on the survivors, but we find her confiding in Jack about her work, stating that she hates Ben, and ultimately siding with the survivors in an attempt to help both her and the castaways escape from the Others.

Lost keeps viewers guessing in large part because they don't know, along the way, who is good and who is bad. Ethan was an Other who infiltrated the survivors by posing as one of them. Rousseau captures Sayid, but later helps him in his efforts. Sayid tortures Sawyer, but later gives him a gun as they work together.

All these guessing games point toward a larger theme that can be found in *Lost*—a definition of good and evil and its role in our lives today.

Is Jack "Jesus"?

Many online sources have argued that Jack is not only trying to fix or save everyone on the island, but that he seems like a Christ-figure. Why? Notice the resemblances:

- Jack's tattoo: "He walks amongst us, but he is not one of us."

- Jack sacrifices himself at the brig so that his friends could live.

- Jack is betrayed by Michael; Jesus was betrayed by Judas.

- Jack performs CPR on Charlie, bringing him back from near death.

- Jack serves as a healer in his doctor role.

- The other survivors look to Jack as their leader.

- Jack leads the survivors to water, just as Jesus claimed to be the water of life (see John 4:10-15).

- Jack's last name is Shephard; Jesus is the good shepherd (John 10:11).

- In "Through the Looking Glass," Jack stands on the edge of a bridge with outstretched arms like Jesus on the cross, complete with the full beard. He then looks up and says, "Lord, forgive me" as he prepares to die. This could be an allusion to the words of Jesus on the cross, "Father, forgive *them*, for they do not know what they are doing" (Luke 23:34, though there is a big difference between "forgive me" and "forgive them").

Yet there are also substantial differences. Unlike Jesus, Jack loses his temper and fails at several points, ending Season Three as a prescription drug addict on the verge of suicide. Though he is a representative of good, he is not without faults. Jack may not really be a Jesus figure, but certainly seems to play one on *Lost*.

What Can Be Found in *Lost*?

The problem of evil is one of the greatest challenges that skeptics bring up to those of the Christian faith. They ask questions such as, "If God really is all-powerful and loving, then why am I suffering this way? Why does a good God allow his creatures, and even his children, to suffer? Why does God allow wars, hunger, violence, and natural disasters? Is God really there at all?"

Jesus made the surprising statement that "the Son of Man must suffer many things" (Luke 9:22). Even Jesus endured pain and suffering during his life. In the Bible, the word "evil" appears over 440 different times. God is familiar with the reality of evil and addresses it directly. God is also intimately familiar with suffering. He addresses it 145 times in Scripture. One of the larger books of the Bible, the book of Job, is given solely to the topic of suffering. The books of Jeremiah and Habakkuk have much to say about it as well. About one-third of the psalms are cries that arise out of doubt, disappointment, or pain. And Jesus experienced the worst of suffering and evil at the hands of others during his crucifixion.

For these reasons, people—even Christians—have their doubts about God. Yet Dr. Erwin Lutzer writes:

> We must be careful about what we say about tragedies. If we say too much, we may err, thinking we can read the fine print of God's purposes. But if we say nothing, we give the impression that there is no message we can learn from calamities. I believe that God does speak through these events, but we must be cautious about thinking we know the details of his agenda.[2]

First, it's important to distinguish between two kinds of evil: moral evil and natural evil. Moral evil results from the actions of free creatures. Murder, rape, and theft are examples. Why doesn't God turn the knife or gun or the murderer into Jell-O? Why doesn't he stuff a person's mouth with cotton every time he or she wants to say hurtful words? He could, but then people would say, "That's not fair. I'm not free to act or make my own decisions." God has given us freedom, and much of the evil in this world comes from the free decisions of fallen human beings.

Natural evil results from natural events such as earthquakes and floods. Of course sometimes moral and natural evil are intermingled, such as when flooding results in the loss of human life. In the plane crash that begins *Lost,* the crash results in death and tragedy, but not as a result of murder or intentional wrongdoing (though we later find out *why* the plane crashed). However, this natural evil caused pain and suffering for many.

Moral evil is also evident in *Lost.* People are shot, lies are told, individuals are kidnapped, and fights break out on a regular basis.

Moral Evil:	Murder, rape, theft, lying, cheating
Natural Evil:	Earthquakes, floods, hurricanes, human disease, famine
Combined:	Poverty due to war, human disease spread through illegal drug use

But what *does* the Bible say about good and evil? First, it acknowledges that both exist. The Bible speaks of both, and encourages and commands those who love God to choose what is right and to live according to his ways. In fact, evil was not part of God's original creation. It was only when the first humans (Adam and Eve) chose to turn against God's ways that evil was introduced into the world (Genesis 3). As C.S. Lewis wrote in *Mere Christianity:*

> Quarrelling means trying to show that the other man is in the wrong. And there would be no sense in trying to do that

unless you and he had some sort of agreement as to what Right and Wrong are; just as there would be no sense in saying that a footballer had committed a foul unless there was some agreement about the rules of football.[3]

How do we define evil? *Evil* could be defined as "the lack of the good." God is absolutely good, and he made an absolutely good world. One of the good aspects of creation is that God gave his creatures free will. It is good to be free. Hardly anyone would say freedom is bad because, if they did, it would be self-defeating because they are exercising their freedom, which they enjoy as a good, in order to say freedom is bad. So freedom is undeniably good.

Yet freedom is also the source of evil, because if you are really free to love God, you are also free *not* to love Him, because forced love is a contradiction in terms. If you are free to worship him, you are free to turn against him. So evil arose from free will.

Freedom is a good thing. God created the good of freedom. And man performs acts of evil when he misuses his freedom.

Second, the existence of evil motivates us to depend on God and his power. In our own strength, we do wrong and live selfishly at times. No power within us can change these facts of life. However, for those who trust in Christ, God forgives these wrongs and provides the Holy Spirit, who empowers them to live according to God's ways. The apostle Paul wrote,

> When you follow the desires of your sinful nature, the results are very clear: sexual immorality, impurity, lustful pleasures, idolatry, sorcery, hostility, quarreling, jealousy, outbursts of anger, selfish ambition, dissension, division, envy, drunkenness, wild parties, and other sins like these. Let me tell you again, as I have before, that anyone living that sort of life will not inherit the Kingdom of God.

> But the Holy Spirit produces this kind of fruit in our lives: love, joy, peace, patience, kindness, goodness, faithfulness, gentleness, and self-control. There is no law against these things!

> Those who belong to Christ Jesus have nailed the passions
> and desires of their sinful nature to his cross and crucified
> them there. Since we are living by the Spirit, let us follow
> the Spirit's leading in every part of our lives. Let us not
> become conceited, or provoke one another, or be jealous of
> one another (Galatians 5:19-26 NLT).

Third, this Earth is not the best of worlds, but it is the world to help us reach the best of all possible worlds. In other words, this life is not all there is. The Bible promises that there is coming a day when evil will end. At the end of time, "no longer will there be any curse" (Revelation 22:3). God has dealt with the sin that began with Adam and Eve and continued though human history by sending Jesus to pay the penalty for sin. Life is now made up of two ultimate choices. We can accept God's remedy for sin, or we can refuse to turn to God and instead, live life in our own power. And evil will end only for all those who have trusted in Christ and eventually go on to live in God's presence in heaven.

Lost provides excellent examples of contrasts between good and evil. Even the most mature believers in Christ are forced to wrestle with issues of right and wrong and the nature of good and evil. However, as Christians, the basis and standard for all good and evil is decided according to the Bible. *Lost* presents the problems caused by sin and evil in the world, and only the Bible provides the *answers* to these problems.

Lost Talk

- What are some of the most difficult portrayals of good and evil you have noticed in *Lost*?

- How do the characters in *Lost* decide what is right and wrong? What basis do they use to determine their beliefs?

- In *Lost*, how do we know which side is the good side and which side is the bad side? In what ways are we led to this conclusion?

LOST on the Bible

EKO: *Hello. I have something I think you should see. If you don't mind, I will begin at the beginning. Long before Christ the king of Judah was a man named Josiah.*

LOCKE: *Boy when you say beginning, you mean beginning.*

EKO: *At that time the temple where the people worshipped was in ruin. And so the people worshipped idols, false gods. And so the kingdom was in disarray. Josiah, since he was a good king, sent his secretary to the treasury and said, "We must rebuild the temple. Give all of the gold to the workers so that this will be done." But when the secretary returned, he had no gold. And when Josiah asked why this was the secretary replied, "We found a book." Do you know this story?*

LOCKE: *No, I'm afraid I don't.*

EKO: *What the secretary had found was an ancient book...the Book of Law. You may know it as the Old Testament. And it was with that ancient book, not with the gold, that Josiah rebuilt the temple. On*

> *the other side of the island we found a place much
> like this, and in this place we found a book.*
>
> (Mr. Eko shows Locke the Holy Bible, which he found
> in the Arrow bunker.)
>
> EKO: *I believe what's inside there will be of great value
>   to you.*
>
> (Locke opens the book, which contains a cutout with a
> section of film.)
>
> —FROM "WHAT KATE DID"

In "What Kate Did," we find the most significant emphasis so far in the series regarding the Bible and its value to the castaways of *Lost*. Eko, a Catholic priest, shares the story of King Josiah, explaining that the survivors from the plane's tail section had found a place similar to the Jewish temple and had found a book similar to the Book of Law found by the temple workers. Yet as with nearly every aspect of *Lost*, there is a twist. The Bible was not considered important because of its words, but because inside the Bible's cover was a splice of film.

No one who has watched *Lost* would deny the Bible is loaded with spiritual meanings, but few have taken the time to investigate what the show says about the Bible itself. Because the Bible is the sole authoritative book of Christianity, it should be of great interest—to Christians and non-Christians—what the show communicates about it.

Addressing the Issue: "I believe what's inside there will be of great value to you."

Lost is certainly not afraid to deal head-on with issues in and about the Bible. The following list includes many of the references to the Bible in the first three seasons:

- Bibles are found by Boone on board a crashed plane in "Deus ex Machina."
- In "The Other 48 Days," a Bible is found in a chest by the tail-end survivors.

- Episode titles "Exodus," "Numbers," and "The 23rd Psalm" are all the titles of books or chapters in the Bible.

- Michael's attorney references the biblical story of David and Goliath in "Adrift."

- Locke names the skeletons discovered in the cave Adam and Eve (names found in the Genesis account) in "House of the Rising Sun."

- Eko and Charlie recite the 23rd Psalm as Yemi's plane is burned in "The 23rd Psalm."

- Claire's baby is named *Aaron*, which is the name of Moses' brother in Exodus.

- Eko, a Catholic priest, observes the biblical practice of baptism when he baptizes Claire and Aaron in "Fire + Water."

- Eko misinterprets the baptism of Jesus by John in "Fire + Water."

- Eko and Charlie begin building a church in "Three Minutes."

- Eko carries a "Jesus Stick" with verses etched into it.

- Eko served Catholic churches in Nigeria and England. He also argues with Yemi in Yemi's Nigerian Catholic church.

- Eko finds Yemi's Bible in the church in "The Cost of Living." The picture of Eko and Yemi as children was found in Isaiah 4 and 5, a chapter about judgment and including the number 4 (some numbers in *Lost* have special significance).

- In "Strangers in a Strange Land," Alex says the Others use "an eye for an eye" as their basis for punishment—this phrase is from the Bible.

- The episode title "Strangers in a Strange Land" could come from the King James translation of Exodus 2:22.

- Cassidy poses as a Bible salesperson in "Left Behind."

- A Bible is shown and the story of Isaac (from the book of Genesis) is discussed in "Catch-22."

- Ben (a biblical name meaning "son") claims that Jacob (another biblical name from Genesis, and the father of Benjamin in Genesis) is the real leader of the island, though who Jacob is has not been fully revealed. Interestingly, Jacob means "he who supplants" in Hebrew, which is a reference to the younger twin's deception of his brother Esau to obtain Esau's inheritance.

- The wine Desmond makes as a monk includes the name *Moriah*, the place where Abraham took Isaac with the intent of sacrificing him.

- Desmond also had a Bible in the Swan station, which is seen on the bed next to *The Third Policeman* in "Man of Science, Man of Faith."

- A Bible is found on Jack's office bookshelf in "A Tale of Two Cities."

- Jack is called *Moses* in "Through the Looking Glass," a biblical name from the Old Testament.

In one interesting scene, Cassidy, a con woman working to help Kate, disguises herself as a Bible salesperson and pretends to be selling Bibles door to door when she is apprehended by a marshal who thought she was Kate. When she talked about the experience later with Kate, she shared that "they questioned me for half an hour. They confiscated my case…he was asking me about selling Bibles…oh, it's a good thing I know how to lie."

Again, the Bible is utilized for a scene, but in a situation that connects it to a con woman lying her way out of trouble. The writers of *Lost* seemingly enjoy creating these stark contrasts, which help keep the viewers intrigued and wondering what will happen next.

Season Two, in many ways, communicates the most biblical

concepts, primarily through the life of Eko. Eko, a drug lord turned priest, carves a Jesus Stick, baptizes infant Aaron and his mother, Claire, and even sets out to build a church. *Lost*'s creators go to great lengths on Eko's Jesus Stick alone to communicate clues about the story's plot, using biblical concepts while doing so:

══ The (Many) Meanings of Eko's Jesus Stick ══

Serious fans of *Lost* know all about Mr. Eko and his Jesus Stick, a rod in which he has etched various Bible verses. The following identifies what is written on each side, along with an analysis of the meanings.

Side 1:

Hab 1:3

John 3:05 (?)

LIFT UP YOUR EYES AND LOOK NORTH

Acts 4:12

Rom 6:12

Gen 13:14

4:8:15:16

Side 2:

23 PSALM

PSALM 144

REVELATION 5:3 (or Revelations :3)

HATETH

Colosians (spelled wrong)

T:4

TITUS:3

One site notes that 9 22 was added during "Live Together, Die Alone," marking the date of the plane crash.[1]

Eko's Jesus Stick Analyzed

The stick or rod is a biblical symbol of authority, as used by a shepherd to lead a flock (Exodus 4:2,20; 7:17 and many other passages). This is especially true of Moses and Aaron (another *Lost* name) and David.

Interestingly, the term *Jesus Stick* was first made famous during the American colonial period, when many ministers were forced to carry a Jesus Stick for safety from potential attackers.[2]

Side 1
Hab 1:3 [Habakkuk 1:3: "Why do you make me look at injustice? Why do you tolerate wrong? Destruction and violence are before me; there is strife, and conflict abounds." A likely reference to Eko's questions about the good and evil he has experienced on the island.]

John 3:05 [A nonstandard way of listing John 3:5, in which Jesus said, "I tell you the truth, no one can enter the kingdom of God unless he is born of water and the Spirit." Probably a reference to the baptism episode in Season Two. However, it has also been observed that "John 3:05" was the compass bearing John Locke used in "Tricia Tanaka Is Dead" to find the other station, and that Eko always called Locke by his first name, John. This also connects with the next phrase about looking to the north. Still another observation is that Episode 3:05, "The Cost of Living," was when Eko was killed by a monster.]

LIFT UP YOUR EYES AND LOOK NORTH [This is, in part, what appears in Genesis 13:14, though no English version of the Bible has this exact phrasing; therefore, possibly a paraphrase. As mentioned above, it is also part of Locke's clues to finding the other station.]

Acts 4:12 ["Salvation is found in no one else, for there is no other name under heaven given to men by which we must be saved." This is a reference to salvation only in Jesus, a redemption Eko looks to during times of trouble. It also contains the *Lost* number 4, along with a combination (12-4=8) that equals another *Lost* number.]

Rom 6:12 ["Do not let sin reign in your mortal body so that you obey its evil desires." This is a reminder to Eko to live with self-control. One theory asks, Could Rom (Romans) 6:12 have something to do with Ethan Rom? One possible anagram of Ethan Rom is "the Roman."[3]]

Gen 13:14 [The LORD said to Abram after Lot had parted from him,

"Lift up your eyes from where you are and look north and south, east and west." This is part of God's promise to Abram (Abraham) regarding his future land of inheritance. It is likely a reference to when Locke and Eko look north to find the other station.]

4:8:15:16 [Part of the *Lost* string of numbers, though not a clear Bible reference. It is implied that the rest of the number string is etched into the stick as well, though unseen in the freeze-frame shots of Eko's Jesus Stick.]

Side 2
23 PSALM [Famous psalm and the name of an episode of *Lost*.]

PSALM 144 [A 15-verse psalm of David that speaks of battle and the blessings of those who belong to God. The reference is likely numerical (15) and a reference to battle.]

REVELATION 5:3 (or Revelations :3) [If it is 5:3, then the book is spelled correctly and refers to these words: "No one in heaven or on earth or under the earth could open the scroll or even look inside it." This clearly refers to opening something, though the analogy is not clear to a specific scene in *Lost*. Is it a reference to the Bible with the film in it? The hatch? Something else? Another interesting twist is that the book of Revelation is also called "the Apocalypse of John," meaning the scripture could be a hint at John Locke seeing into the future. Ironically enough, the apostle John was banished to the Isle of Patmos when he wrote the book of Revelation.]

HATETH [Is this the King James English word "hateth"? This makes sense on the surface and is our preference since we've seen no better solution. The problem is that this form is used 30 times in the King James Bible, and we are not told which verse is in mind. The closest match is Proverbs 13:24: "He that spareth his rod hateth his son: but he that loveth him chasteneth him betimes." Is this a reference to Eko's Jesus Stick (rod)? HATETH might also be a reference to John 15:23: "He that hateth me hateth my Father also." Incidentally (maybe?) this is the twenty-third line of John 15. Another idea is a possible connection with Psalm 23:4: "Your rod and your staff, they comfort me."]

Colosians [First, Eko spells the name of the apostle Paul's letter incorrectly, leaving out an "s." Second, no specific verse is mentioned, so it's hard to be clear on what this inscription means.]

T:4 [This is the most mysterious biblical reference on Eko's Jesus Stick. The only possible matching Bible books are 1 and 2 Thessalonians, 1 and 2 Timothy, and Titus. Of those, only 1 Thessalonians and 1 and 2 Timothy have four chapters. First Thessalonians 4 has 18 verses and is about living to please God and the Lord's future coming. First Timothy 4 has 16 verses (a *Lost* number) and is about instructions to the young pastor Timothy regarding people who follow wrong teaching and the need for Timothy to stand strong. Second Timothy 4 has 22 verses and is about preaching the Word and fighting the good fight of faith. Our personal thought is that T:4 refers to 1 Timothy 4 because 1) it is a message for a young church leader (like Eko); 2) it is one of only three biblical options; 3) the number of verses in the chapter also happens to be one of the main *Lost* numbers.]

TITUS:3 [Titus 3 is about doing what is good. It also contains 15 verses, again hitting one of the *Lost* numbers.]

Additional Notes: There are also a numerically significant seven markings on each side of Eko's stick (at least originally). Also, after Eko's death, what happened to the Jesus Stick? Locke kept the stick in his backpack. As noted by one observer, Locke took this backpack into the submarine he blew up and returned without it.[4] The famous Jesus Stick was likely blown up in the blast (that is, if Locke really blew up the submarine).

What Can Be Found in *Lost*?

Those who value the Bible can find numerous examples of biblical themes in *Lost* that are both insightful and instructive. For instance, when the story of Isaac is discussed, it opens opportunities to talk openly about an important account within the Jewish and Christian traditions. Also, when Eko and Charlie recite Psalm 23, many Christians found themselves resonating with the words of hope found in the passage. During these and many other times the Bible is mentioned, *Lost* opens doors into subject matters that are sometimes difficult to talk about otherwise with those who do not read or care about the Bible.

However, a word of caution must also be cast. *Lost* is not attempting to communicate accurate theology or provide a persuasive message for Christianity. The series sometimes misinterprets biblical teachings to fit a given episode's plot. While this is not the norm, two specific quotes have frustrated those with a high view of the biblical text because of their misinformed interpretations.

Biblical Names Used in *Lost*		
Name	**Use in *Lost***	**Use in the Bible**
Adam and Eve	Names of skeletons in the cave	First people in Genesis
Aaron	Claire's son	Brother of Moses
Sarah	Jack Shephard's ex-wife	Abraham's wife
Isaac	Isaac Uluru, Australian faith healer	Abraham and Sarah's son
Jacob	Leader of the Others	Leader of 12 tribes of Israel
Rachel	Used of four different characters, especially Tom Brennan's wife and Rachel Carlson, sister of Juliet	Wife of Jacob
Benjamin	Operation leader of the Others	Son of Jacob, leader of one of the 12 tribes of Israel
Dan/Daniel	Multiple characters, especially Danny Pickett, one of the Others	Dan was a son of Jacob and tribal leader. Daniel was a prophet and author of a Bible book
Michael	Father of Walt	A lead angel

Naomi	Woman who parachutes onto the island	Mother-in-law of Ruth, after whom a Bible book is named
Ethan	One of the Others	A cymbal player in King David's court
James	Sawyer's other name	A common Bible name, including the brother of Jesus and two of Jesus' disciples
John	John Locke	Common name, especially the apostle John and John the Baptist
Elizabeth	Name of Desmond's boat	Mother of John the Baptist and cousin of Mary, mother of Jesus
Tom/Thomas	Tom is one of the Others; Thomas was Claire's ex-boyfriend	A disciple of Jesus

The first and most blatant of these two errors is found in a statement from Eko regarding the baptism of Jesus in "Water + Fire." When Claire asks him about baptism, he answers, "It is said that when John the Baptist baptized Jesus the skies opened up and a dove flew down from the sky. This told John something...that he had cleansed this man of all his sins. That he had freed him. Heaven came much later."

Lost is completely incorrect in stating that Jesus had been cleansed of his sins, because he was sinless. Jesus himself challenged his enemies by asking, "Can any of you prove me guilty of sin?" (John 8:46).

Also, it is biblically incorrect to say this event told John something about Jesus. John himself stated:

> I saw the Spirit come down from heaven as a dove and remain on him. I would not have known him, except that the one who sent me to baptize with water told me, "The man on whom you see the Spirit come down and remain is

he who will baptize with the Holy Spirit." I have seen and I testify that this is the Son of God (John 1:32-34).

Because Jesus never sinned, obviously he did not need to be cleansed through baptism. So why was he baptized? There are several reasons:

1. To indicate he was consecrated by God and officially approved by him "to fulfill all righteousness" (Matthew 3:15).
2. For John the Baptist to publicly announce the arrival of the Messiah (John 1:32-34).
3. For Jesus to identify himself with our sins and become our substitute (2 Corinthians 5:21).
4. As an example for his followers to follow (Matthew 28:19).

Unfortunately, in this case, Eko says much more than the Bible does. Nowhere in these verses is there an indication that Jesus was forgiven of sins. In fact, the Bible teaches quite the opposite—that Jesus was without sin. The New Testament notes that "we do not have a high priest who is unable to sympathize with our weaknesses, but we have one who has been tempted in every way, just as we are—*yet was without sin*" (Hebrews 4:15). This is a key Christian teaching the writers of *Lost* completely missed.

The second biblical misquote in *Lost* deals more with a concept than with a specific chapter or verse. When Bernard decides to build a signal on the beach in "SOS" he runs into Eko and quips, "Everybody on this island is building something. I'm trying to get us saved."

Eko answers, "People are saved in different ways, Bernard."

Frustrated, Bernard remarks, "I think I liked you better when you just hit people with your stick."

Though a humorous scene, Eko's multiple-roads-to-heaven approach does not line up with what the Bible communicates about salvation. Even one of the verses on Eko's Jesus Stick, Acts 4:12, clearly notes that "salvation is found in no one else, for there is no other name under heaven given to men by which we must be saved." The New Testament clearly states that faith in Jesus Christ is the only way to become saved and enter heaven.

On this issue, *Lost* reflects the common view of our culture, but certainly not the view of the real Jesus, who lived 2000 years ago. For instance, in the recent Robert Ludlum series novel, *The Bourne Betrayal*, Jason Bourne tracks a terrorist into the Blue Mosque, joining in prayer on his own prayer mat:

> Bourne said the Muslim prayers, his forehead pressed to the carpet he had just bought. He was perfectly sincere in his prayers, feeling the centuries of history etched in the stone, marble, gold leaf, and lapis with which the mosque had been constructed and fervently embellished. Spirituality came in many guises, was called by many names, but they all spoke directly to his heart in a language as old as time.[5]

This all-gods-are-the-same-God attitude is not the perspective of Jesus or of the Bible. A brief sampling of the beliefs of various religions illustrates just a small portion of the many vast differences that exist among the various views of God:[6]

Krishna	Mix of polytheism (many gods) and impersonal pantheism (all is God). The universe is eternal.
Zoroaster	One good god and one evil god (religious dualism).
Buddha	God is not relevant; essentially agnostic. Some would even say atheistic.
Muhammad	God cannot have a son.
Jesus Christ	God does have a son.
Joseph Smith (founder of Mormonism)	Essentially polytheistic. Taught that there are many gods and that the father of Christ has a human body.
Baha'u'llah (of the Baha'i faith)	God and the universe, which is an emanation of God, are co-eternal.

(Source: http://www.spotlightministries.org.uk/plural.htm)

In the words of Jesus, he is *"the* way and *the* truth and *the* life" (John

14:6). The idea that Jesus is the only way to receive forgiveness from God originated in Jesus' own words.

In Eko's dialogue with Bernard, some may argue that Eko is speaking of being saved in relation to Bernard's plans for physical rescue from the beach. However, the multiple-meanings approach of *Lost* and the fact that this dialogue was in the context of Eko building a church versus Bernard placing words on the beach indicates that more was at stake than whether the wood was more important for Bernard's or Eko's purposes.

Overall, however, even those who take the Bible very literally should be impressed that *Lost* includes numerous biblical references and usually uses its biblical insights in positive ways. Regardless of your personal perspectives, it is clear that *Lost* is loaded with spiritual meaning and biblical information that continues to spark debate and controversy among viewers.

Lost Talk

- Why do you think the creators of *Lost* use the Bible and biblical themes so much in the series?

- In what ways does *Lost* use biblical concepts in a positive manner? In what ways does it use them negatively?

- How do you feel when *Lost* uses a biblical concept in a way that is different from the intended meaning of the Bible? Why do you feel this way?

LOST on Dreams and Visions

CHARLIE: *So you ready to tell me what you saw this morning?*

DESMOND: *Aye.*

CHARLIE: *Right. So how's it happen this time? Come on, Des. You can tell me. I can take it.*

DESMOND: *What I saw Charlie was…Claire and her baby getting into a helicopter. A helicopter that… that lifts off…leaves this island…*

CHARLIE: *A rescue helicopter? On this beach? This island? That's what you saw? We're getting bloody rescued! I thought you were gonna tell me I was gonna die again! Are you sure?*

DESMOND: *You are, Charlie.*

CHARLIE: *Wait. What?*

DESMOND: *If you don't, none of it will happen. There won't be any rescue. I'm sorry, brother, but this time…this time you have to die.*

—FROM "GREATEST HITS"

Season Three repeatedly portrays Desmond seeing "flashes" (future visions) of Charlie dying. He first saves Charlie by rescuing Claire. Later, Desmond helps keep an arrow from hitting Charlie—an arrow that he foresaw being launched from a trap on the island. But toward the end of Season Three, we find Desmond telling Charlie, "This time you have to die."

But can we trust our dreams and visions? Do people really have dreams that predict future events? These questions are definitely worth considering.

Addressing the Issue: "You get any flashes?"

In addition to Desmond's flashes, *Lost* presents many other forms of dreams. Fan Web sites have devoted enormous efforts toward chronicling each one, with well over 30 listed to date. While there are too many to list individually here, we can divide these dreams and visions into the following categories:

1. Night dreams: The normal kind of dreams, such as Claire's dreams in Season One.
2. Day dreams/visions: People have dreams or visions during the day, such as Jack's dad and Kate's horse.
3. Hallucinations: At least one dream can be classified as a hallucination—when Boone dreamt about Shannon dying after Locke put a paste on Boone's head wound.
4. Desmond's "flashes": In Season Three, Desmond experiences a series of "flashes," similar to prophecies, after the hatch explosion.
5. The "flash forward": In the Season Three finale, "Through the Looking Glass," Jack and Kate are involved in some type of "flash forward." Whether this is what really happens or is simply a dream or potential future event has not yet been revealed.

Flashes in Season Three

"When I turned that key…my life…flashed before my eyes. And then I was back in the jungle. Still on this bloody island. But those flashes, Charlie? Those flashes…they didn't stop."
—DESMOND, IN "FLASHES BEFORE YOUR EYES"

"So, you're telling me you saw a flash of Claire drowning this morning. That's how you knew how to save her?"
—CHARLIE, IN "FLASHES BEFORE YOUR EYES"

"Desmond…said I was going to die. He…e…e tells me he has these flashes, visions…whatever. And in them, I always die."
—CHARLIE, IN "TRICIA TANAKA IS DEAD"

"Doesn't work like that. I only see flashes."
—DESMOND, IN "EXPOSÉ"

"In one of your puzzle flashes?"
—HURLEY, IN "CATCH-22"

"The flashes don't happen exactly how I saw them. The picture changes. I was supposed to let you die, Charlie."
—DESMOND, IN "CATCH-22"

"You've forgotten what's at stake here. She's just another one of your flashes, who's getting an arrow in the neck this time."
—CHARLIE, IN "D.O.C."

"Wait. You had one of your flashes again, didn't you?"
—CHARLIE, IN "GREATEST HITS"

"No your…your flashes."
—CHARLIE, IN "GREATEST HITS"

"You get any flashes?"
—CHARLIE, IN "THROUGH THE LOOKING GLASS"

Sometimes the creators of *Lost* do not define whether an event is a dream or really takes place. This keeps the viewers (and characters) guessing as to what they have seen. One of the earliest examples of this was when Jack "saw" his father on the island. His father had died in Sydney, Australia, and was supposed to be on the plane in a coffin, but continues to show up in a suit and tie along the beach or in the jungle.

Did Jack really see his father? Or was he hallucinating? The audience is never told. To complicate matters further, Jack later discovers another part of the plane in the jungle, including his father's casket. He opens it to find it is empty!

Flashbacks in the episode "White Rabbit" hint that the body of Jack's father may have been removed before the flight's takeoff, but we are never told for certain. He may show up again later, either dead or alive. It wouldn't be the first time, since we have already seen Locke's dad show up in Season Three.

I See Dead People

- Jack spots his dad twice and hears his voice on a third occasion.
- Both Eko and Locke interact with Yemi in "The Cost of Living."
- Eko sees Ana-Lucia in a vision in "?".
- Locke speaks with Boone in "Deus Ex Machina."
- Ben (as a child) saw his dead mother twice in "The Man Behind the Curtain."

In "Special" we find another Season One dream at work—this time via Claire's diary. Charlie decides to read it and discovers that she wrote, "I had that weird dream again, the one with the Black Rock I can't get away from. I try to leave but it won't let me." Charlie remembers that Sayid mentioned a black rock on the French woman's map and hopes to use this dream clue to find Claire. She returns on her own, but the

Black Rock ends up becoming an important location on *Lost* later in the season as a pirate ship rather than a physical rock.

In an interesting variation, *Lost* also uses a dream to tell the story of how Sawyer's parents died. In this case, the dream is not used to tell the future, but rather to tell viewers something significant about the past that influences the story of Sawyer, and later, other characters in the series.

Hurley even sees "Dave" in his mind, though we later discover that it is due to a psychological disorder in which he is seeing another personality. But perhaps the most bizarre use of dreams and visions in *Lost* are the occasions when the castaways communicate with the dead or the missing. Walt appears to Shannon in a dream in "Man of Science, Man of Faith," though he is missing from among the survivors. But is this a dream or not? The third time Shannon sees Walt, Sayid sees him as well. The evidence is that they really saw Walt (or some form of Walt) rather than a dream. Yet the way the scene is portrayed leaves viewers trying to figure out what happened.

The Newspaper Clipping

In the flash-forward scenes in "Through the Looking Glass," Jack reads an obituary and attends the funeral of a man who died. An integral part of the mystery of *Lost*, serious fans have put tremendous effort into determining what the article said and who it is about. The best freeze-frame transcriptions appear to read:

> The body of Jo…[unreadable]…[a]ntham of
> New York was discovered shortly after 4
> a.m. in the…[unreadable]…of Grand
> Avenue. Ted [last name], [a door]man at The
> Tower…[unreadable]…heard loud
> noises…[unreadable]…antham's loft.
> [unreadable]…[sa]fety, he co[nfessed]
> [unreadable]…discovered the
> [unreadable]…a beam in the
> [unreadable]…[ac]cordin[g]…[unreadable]…[1]

Interestingly, the article that the episode's newspaper prop is based on is from the April 5, 2007 edition of the *Los Angeles Times*, which was first reported by the *Times* itself on May 24, 2007. Theories range from Michael (due to the location of the funeral) to Ben Linus or even a new unknown character. Only time will tell who guessed right regarding this mysterious flash-forward.

An example of visions of the dead occurs in "Further Instructions"— Locke speaks with Boone in a vision. While some would consider this necromancy (speaking with the dead), the scene is portrayed in such a way that we are uncertain whether this is the case or Locke is simply hallucinating. Later, Locke uses the clues in the vision to find Arrow Station, confusing viewers even more as to whether Locke really tapped into the supernatural or not.

What Can Be Found in *Lost*?

This concept of dreams, visions, and even flashes is one that finds many parallels in the Bible. The words "dream" and "dreams" appear about 70 times in the Bible, in various contexts. God spoke through the dream of an Egyptian leader named Abimelech to command him to return Sarah to her husband Abraham (Genesis 20:3). God also spoke to Jacob in a dream at Bethel to assure him of his future blessings (Genesis 28:10-17). A full list includes:

Person	Dream	Reference
Abimelech	Dream to return Sarah to Abraham	Genesis 20:3
Jacob	Dream about future blessings	Genesis 28:10-17
Joseph (2)	Two dreams about his family bowing to him as leader	Genesis 37
Cupbearer and Baker (2)	Three branches and three baskets	Genesis 40

Pharaoh's dreams	Seven cows and seven heads of grain; called one dream in two forms	Genesis 41
One of Gideon's enemies	Dream of bread, symbolic of losing in battle	Judges 7:12-14
Solomon	Dream of asking God for wisdom	1 Kings 3:15
Nebuchad-nezzar (2)	Dream of a statue and dream of a tree	Daniel 2; 4
Daniel	Dream of four beasts	Daniel 7
Joseph, husband of Mary (4)	Dream to take Mary as his wife; flee with family to Egypt; return from Egypt; settle in Galilee	Matthew 1:20; 2:13, 19,22
Pilate's wife	Dream about Jesus as warning for Pilate not to do anything to him	Matthew 27:19

In total, 17 specific dreams are described in the Bible.[2] They had specific meanings, were revealed to both believers and nonbelievers in God, and contained very real-world results (such as Joseph leaving Bethlehem to avert the death of baby Jesus). However, the Bible is also clear that not every dream has a specific message to communicate. Ecclesiastes 5:3 notes, "As a dream comes when there are many cares, so the speech of a fool when there are many words." Dreams can also result from what we are thinking about during the day or before we fall asleep. It would be very unhealthy and possibly even dangerous to live as if every dream we have has a significant meaning we must act upon.

Further, there are numerous visions listed in the Bible, usually by prophets. Visions could be one of two types: true or false. There is no middle ground in the Bible—no one had some true visions and some false ones. In fact, the Bible condemns those who claim to see visions from God but in reality do not. The prophet Jeremiah wrote, "I have heard what the prophets say who prophesy lies in my name. They say, 'I had a dream! I had a dream!' How long will this continue in the hearts of these lying prophets, who prophesy the delusions of their own minds?" (Jeremiah 23:25-26).

So there are visions, dreams, and prophecies in the Bible, but how do we know which are true and of God and which are not? The Bible provides two tests we can use. The first is found in Deuteronomy 18. There, God speaks through Moses, saying,

> You may say to yourselves, "How can we know when a message has not been spoken by the LORD?" If what a prophet proclaims in the name of the LORD does not take place or come true, that is a message the LORD has not spoken. That prophet has spoken presumptuously. Do not be afraid of him (verses 21-22).

The first guideline is that if the dream or vision does not come true, then we are not to listen to the person who claims to have had the dream. If God has perfect knowledge, then a dream that allegedly comes from God would not be inaccurate.

For instance, Jeanne Dixon was declared as a prophet by many because she supposedly predicted John F. Kennedy's assassination. However, she also predicted that Russia would be the first nation to land a person on the moon, that World War III would begin in 1954, and that Fidel Castro would be overthrown in 1970. Psychics are not 100 percent accurate.

The second principle provided in the Bible regards the allegiance of the person giving the dream or vision. Deuteronomy 13 states:

> If a prophet, or one who foretells by dreams, appears among you and announces to you a miraculous sign or wonder, and if the sign or wonder of which he has spoken takes place, and he says, "Let us follow other gods" (gods you have not known) "and let us worship them," you must not listen to the words of that prophet or dreamer. The LORD your God is testing you to find out whether you love him with all your heart and with all your soul (verses 1-3).

Here we are told that even if a vision does come true, if the dreamer teaches us to serve or worship other gods, then that person must be ignored. Why? These verses share that it is because God is testing his people and making sure they love him above all else.

There are many true visions and prophecies that were given by God's prophets, such as Jeremiah, Isaiah, Ezekiel, Daniel, and others. To get some idea of the extent of the prophetic material in the Bible, here are some key statistics:

- Approximately 27 percent of the entire Bible contains prophetic material. Half of those prophecies have already been fulfilled, and half of them remain to be fulfilled.
- Of the Old Testament's 23,210 verses, 6641 contain prophetic material, or 28.5 percent.
- Of the New Testament's 7914 verses, 1,711 contain prophetic material, or 21.5 percent.
- Of the Bible's 31,124 verses, 8352 contain prophetic material.
- 1800 verses deal with the second coming of Christ.
- In the New Testament, 318 verses deal with the second coming of Christ.
- Every twenty-fifth Bible verse in the New Testament refers to the second coming.[3]

What is found in *Lost* is a very spiritual interpretation of dreams and future flashes that causes viewers to ask tough questions that those who follow Christ need to know how to handle. A look at the mentions of dreams and visions in the Bible reveals that though God sometimes uses these methods to communicate, the most reliable form of communication we have from God is found in the words of the Bible itself.

In addition, when dreams are given by God, they will never contradict information already found in the Bible. In other words, God would not contradict himself by writing that Jesus is God's son, and later reveal to someone that Jesus was merely a great teacher. The two statements would cause God to be in conflict with himself.

It's true that in modern times, some people in closed countries and areas with no missionaries have claimed to have received visions of Jesus and have converted to Christianity. But such experiences are very much the exception, and aren't everyday occurrences. For people to place heavy symbolic meaning on every dream—as in *Lost*—is a practice for television, not real life.

Lost Talk

- What role do you think dreams play in our lives?

- Why do people sometimes become concerned about their dreams? He you experienced this before?

- Can God speak to us today in dreams or visions? On what basis can we evaluate whether God is the one speaking to us or not?

LOST on Leadership

SAYID: *I'm not taking them to the tower. You are.*

JACK: *Excuse me?*

SAYID: *You're not staying behind.*

JACK: *This was my idea.*

SAYID: *And I'm perfectly capable of executing it.*

JACK: *I owe them!*

SAYID: *What are you more concerned about—killing the Others, or getting our people off this island? This afternoon you said you were our leader. It's time for you to act like one. Lead them to the radio tower, Jack. And then take us all home.*

—FROM "GREATEST HITS"

In "Greatest Hits," Sayid confronts Jack about the motives behind his decision making. The Others had captured, hurt, and chased down Jack in ways that had sparked a desire for revenge. Jack was no longer content to get off of the island; he wanted to destroy the Others in the process.

Sayid, in contrast, continued to keep a clear mind and remained focused on the issue at hand. For the group to escape the island and the Others, decisive leadership was needed both at the beach, where a trap had been set, and for the journey to the radio tower. He did not attempt to order Jack around, but appealed to Jack's role as a leader. In Sayid's words, "This afternoon you said you were our leader. It's time for you to act like one."

This scene causes us to consider the complexities of leadership, especially during difficult situations. What traits mark a successful leader? How does a leader "lead"? What are the differences between good leaders and bad ones? *Lost* provides several contexts in which certain individuals take charge and others follow. But what factors determine who leads and who follows?

Addressing the Issue: "It's time for you to act like one."

A common definition is that a leader is someone with influence or someone with followers. Among the castaways in *Lost*, Jack Shephard acts as the primary leader, but several other characters emerge as leaders throughout the series to provide additional perspectives on leadership. A look at the characteristics of some of these *Lost* leaders provides us with several insights about the characteristics of leaders. We also see both strengths and weaknesses among these leaders.

For example, Jack entered his island life with several key leadership strengths. He is one of few survivors with a graduate education. As a trained medical doctor, he was able to keep his emotions stable while treating fellow survivors who had various injuries, including some life-threatening ones. Likewise, his youthfulness, self-confidence, and ability to build friendships among the castaways helped to quickly position him as a source of help for those around him.

Jack is not without his weaknesses, however. Though extremely intelligent, his stubbornness sometimes causes problems for him and the other castaways. At one point, he pushes himself so hard that Kate dilutes sleeping pills in his drinking water to make him rest. On another occasion Jack prepares to amputate Boone's leg in order to save his life, until Boone himself becomes conscious enough to tell him not to do it. Other times, Jack's stubbornness causes others to avoid him, leaving him lonely in the process.

Another example of leadership is found in the character of Sayid. A former Iraqi soldier and assistant to the CIA, he brings plenty of military and electronics expertise to the island. In fact, he is one of the only other individuals besides Jack who is able to remain calm during extreme situations, allowing him the opportunity to influence even Jack's decisions for the group. Sayid's technological skills make him a valuable resource when radios or phones become available, creating unique windows of opportunity for leadership at key points in the series. Interestingly, Sayid is also portrayed as having no problem with Jack being in leadership above him. Sayid provides a secondary leadership role that becomes critical at strategic moments, especially when Jack is no longer with the main group on the island.

Yet Sayid is not without his imperfections. As one who formerly inflicted torture on others, he sometimes comes across as cold and uncaring, though we see at other times that this is not truly the case. The cultural differences as both a former Iraqi soldier and as the only Muslim also makes acceptance by the other survivors more difficult.

An odd type of leadership personality is found in the character of Sawyer. He is seen as a "bad boy" from the start, surprising everyone by using a handgun to shoot a polar bear that could have harmed the survivors. Though the people were thankful for the rescue, concerns were immediately raised about the fact he had a gun and had not told anyone else about it. This, of course, marks much of Sawyer's later leadership. He becomes known as a selfish castaway who steps up to help only when it brings personal benefit. As the series progresses, however, we also discover Sawyer's resourcefulness. He hunts and provides food for the group. He scavenges many medical supplies and other items of value to the castaways. He later helps distribute firearms and is known as one of the few people able to adequately use them.

As a former con man, Sawyer is seen by many as trouble, but nonetheless they also recognize him as a leader who is sometimes necessary for various purposes. An intriguing transformation takes place in "Left Behind," when Hurley tells Sawyer that the survivors are gathering to vote whether to banish Sawyer from the rest of the group. Sawyer catches fish, hunts boar with Desmond, and even takes a blanket to Claire and tries to be nice to Aaron. When Sawyer finds out that Hurley had made up the story about the voting, we find an angry Sawyer who has learned a lesson in the process. In the end he asks:

> SAWYER: *What if I don't want to be the leader?*
>
> HURLEY: *You know, I don't think Jack wanted it either.*
> *Sucks for you, dude.*

We ultimately find in Sawyer a guy who doesn't desire to be a leader but finds himself in positions where he must lead. The shift changes his attitude, and ultimately, his actions.

Other leaders emerge at various points in *Lost* as well. For instance, Boone personally sought leadership early on in "White Rabbit" in his tirade against Jack:

> You think you're all noble and heroic for coming after me? I was fine. You're not the only one who knows what to do around here, you know that? I run a business. Who appointed you our savior, huh? What gives you the right? Look at me. Hey, I'm talking to you. Look at me, Jack. Where are you going? Hey, where are you going? Hey!

Boone's youthfulness and pre-island life of affluence caused him problems early on. However, we later see him working together with others (most notably, Locke) as he learns that teamwork is required for survival on the island.

Ana-Lucia brought her authoritarian attitude to the island with her, alienating most people in the process of becoming the leader of the tail-end survivors. Always one for action, she is seen looking for guns, interrogating people, and even working to build an army with Jack.

Michael also provided leadership early in the series through his construction of showers and a raft. But then he betrayed his fellow castaways. Even Ben Linus, leader of the Others, has shown leadership traits, albeit in controlling and evil ways, in his operational direction of those around him.

Lost on **Leadership**

"Patience, the quality which you lack, GL12, is the hallmark of a leader."

—Locke, in "Walkabout"

"Because I'm not a leader."

—Jack, in "White Rabbit"

"Because a leader can't lead until he knows where he's going."

—Locke, in "White Rabbit"

"Everybody wants me to be a leader until I make a decision that they don't like."

—Jack, in "Exodus, Part 3"

"You are a leader, a great man, but this…this makes you lonely, and frightened, and angry."

—Achara, in "Stranger in a Strange Land"

"What if I don't want to be the leader?"

—Sawyer, in "Left Behind"

"It wasn't a con, dude. If you're gonna be our temporary leader, you need to do some damage control."

—Hurley, in "Left Behind"

"You probably think I'm the leader of this little community. But that's not entirely true. We all answer to someone, John."

—Ben, in "The Man Behind the Curtain"

"Jack's too busy leading to even talk to me. I just wanna help. Please?"

—Hurley, in "Through the Looking Glass"

"I'm going to lead my people up to the radio tower…and I'm gonna make a call…and I'm gonna get them all rescued… every one of them."

—Jack, in "Through the Looking Glass"

What Can Be Found in *Lost*?

Leadership examples, both positive and negative, abound in *Lost*. But what spiritual principles regarding leadership can be found?

To adequately respond to this question, we must first define what we mean by *spiritual* leadership. In other words, is there any difference between spiritual leadership, or distinctly Christian leadership, and other types of leadership?

J. Oswald Sanders, in the classic book *Spiritual Leadership*, wrote,

> Jesus was a revolutionary, not in the guerilla warfare sense, but in His teaching on leadership. The term *servant* speaks everywhere of low prestige, low respect, low honor. Most people are not attracted to such a low-value role. When Jesus used the term, however, it was a synonym for greatness. And that was a revolutionary idea.[1]

The Bible is filled with examples of servant leadership. Moses, the man who helped free the Israelites from Egyptian captivity, was called God's servant. David, who was a man after God's own heart and a king of Israel, was also known as God's servant. Mary, the mother of Jesus, when told that she would give birth to Christ, said, "I am the Lord's servant" (Luke 1:38).

Some Major Leaders Mentioned in the Bible	
Leader	**Leadership Role**
Adam	Caretaker of the Garden of Eden
Noah	Led building of the ark and brought his family and animals through the flood
Abraham	Followed God's call to move to a new land with his family
Joseph	Led Egypt under Pharaoh's rule and forgave his brothers for selling him into slavery
Moses	Led the Israelites out of Egyptian captivity
Joshua	Led the nation of Israel into the Promised Land
David	Led the military of Israel and became the nation's second king

Esther	Spoke to the king of Persia on behalf of the Jews to spare them from persecution and possible extinction
Mary, mother of Jesus	Loyally followed God in giving birth to Jesus and raising him despite ridicule from those in her community
Peter	Boldly taught about the resurrection of Jesus and served as a key leader in the early church
Paul	Traveled as a missionary to start churches across the Roman Empire despite frequent persecution

We find throughout Scripture, then, that spiritual leadership is dependent upon God and motivated in service to others. How does this compare with what we find communicated through the characters of *Lost?*

On the positive side, we find leadership that serves others—such as Jack's medical care. Sayid serves the castaways by sharing his knowledge of many technological matters. Hurley contributes through building positive relationships among the group. Sawyer slowly learns that leading is about helping others, not himself.

Benjamin Linus offers a clear example of a person providing self-focused leadership. He frequently lies, even to his closest followers, in order to manipulate them into doing what he desires. He has yet to be seen as giving of himself to help others. His plans are closely guarded—to the point that Locke forces Ben to take him to see Jacob. However, even in this case, Ben shoots Locke and leaves him for dead.

════ Christ's Leadership Model ════

"God's grace to us led Christ to his death. Jesus did not come into the world to gain status or political power, but to suffer and die so that we could have eternal life. If it is difficult for us to identify with Christ's servant attitude, perhaps we need to evaluate our own motives. Are we more interested in power or participation, domination or service, getting or giving?"
—FROM *The Handbook of Bible Application*[2]

What we can learn from the survivors in *Lost* is that, first and foremost, leadership is not easy. A person can't just say, "I'm a leader" and expect others to follow. Leadership must be earned. If there are no followers, you are not a leader.

Second, leadership is proven most in times of struggle. Following the plane crash, chaos ensued. Sayid and Jack were the only people to keep their cool during this time and help those around them. This helped others to recognize them as leaders.

Third, leadership is a team sport. Leaders in *Lost* who have chosen to lead alone have often ended up alone. This has been seen with Ana-Lucia especially, and with Sawyer at times. Ben has also been questioned by his followers as more of his leadership faults become evident.

Lost offers great insights into leadership functioning at its best and its worst, just as we would expect from one of television's top drama series. However, when it comes to *spiritual* leadership, there are certain values in the series that are neglected—values we can discover more from the Bible than from culture.

Lost Talk

- How would you define what it means to be a leader? What is the difference between a good leader and a bad one?

- In what ways is spiritual leadership different from other kinds of leadership?

- Why do you think many people do not desire to be a leader? How do you feel about being a leader?

- What are some ways Jesus serves as a role model of leadership?

LOST on Numbers

KEN: *I'm an accountant; I believe in numbers. Hey, where'd you get them, anyway?*

HURLEY: *What?*

KEN: *The winning numbers. What'd you use— somebody's birthday, phone number?*

HURLEY: *No, it's nothing, it's something that I…*

KEN: *What?*

HURLEY: *That's it. It's not the money, it's the numbers. The numbers are cursed. Dude, don't look at me like that. I'm not crazy. This is real.*

KEN: *C'mon Hugo, listen to yourself…the numbers aren't cursed. You know there is no such thing as a…*

(A body falls past the window.)

—FROM "NUMBERS"

Perhaps nothing has driven more speculation and discussion about *Lost* than this mysterious sequence of numbers: 4-8-15-16-23-42. It began with Hurley using the number to win a lottery. He later sees the same numbers on Rousseau's map (seven different times!).

Through Hurley's flashbacks, we discover that he has experienced a string of bad luck since winning the lottery, leading him to believe the numbers are cursed. By the time he sees the same numbers on the hatch, he has convinced himself that this is definitely the case.

By the second season, we learn that this same series of numbers must be input into the computer inside the Swan station every 108 minutes to keep an unknown disaster from occurring (108 is also the sum of this string of numbers). If the numbers are not entered in time, a series of glyphs appear in preparation for a doomsday disaster. The crew in the Swan station is supposed to be replaced every 540 days (108 x 5), which means that each crew will enter the numbers at least 7200 times.[1]

Throughout the series, viewers are compelled to wonder if there are special powers in these numbers. Are they really cursed? Hurley and others struggle with this issue over multiple episodes amidst endless theories regarding the significance of these numbers in *Lost* and even in real life.

Addressing the Issue: "The numbers are cursed."

Are the numbers really cursed? Is there a special power at work within the numbers themselves? When things start going wrong after Hurley wins the lottery, he asks these same questions himself. In fact, his curiosity about the numbers is how he ended up on Oceanic Flight 815 in the first place. After spotting the same numbers seven different times on Rousseau's map (Rousseau is a woman who has lived alone on the island for 16 years), Hurley begins to worry even more. His fears come to a peak at the hatch, where he once again sees the dreaded 4-8-15-16-23-42.

Do the Numbers Really Work?

After the episode "Numbers" aired on March 2, 2005, numerous people used the *Lost* string of numbers as lottery entries. According to the *Pittsburgh Tribune-Review*, within three days, this set of numbers was tried over 500 times by local lottery players. In the same period, over 200 people in

Michigan alone used the sequence for the Mega Millions lottery, and by October, thousands had tried the numbers for the multistate Powerball lottery.[2]

Lost also sneaks this sequence of numbers into seemingly random junctures throughout the series. Entire fan sites are devoted to spotting and analyzing the vast number of both intentional and unintentional references in each episode. In fact, when the episode "Numbers" aired in March 2005, within hours a fan registered the domain name 4815162342.com to host a message board site for number-theory speculation. The site hosts 50,340 registered users at the time of this writing. Fans can even buy online their own T-shirts sporting the number 4815162342.[3]

The Numbers in Sequence (A Brief Sampling):

- Danielle's notes contained the numbers written seven times in "Numbers."

- In "Numbers," Leonard speaks the numbers in the mental hospital, having learned them from Sam Toomey while serving in the navy in the South Pacific.

- Winning lottery numbers for Hurley in "Numbers."

- In "Numbers," the transmission of the numbers led Rousseau to the island.

- When Hurley's car broke down, his speedometer (in km/h) was shown going from 16 to 15 to 8 to 4. The dashboard also displayed a temperature of 23 degrees Celsius and the odometer read 42 km in "Exodus, Part 2."

- In "Exodus, Part 2," when Hurley rides past six players of a girls' soccer team in an airport, each uniform has one of the numbers on it.

- The numbers appear on the entrance hatch to the Swan station in "Exodus, Part 2."

- The numbers are seen on the medicine that Desmond injects into his arm in "Man of Science, Man of Faith."

- The numbers are entered into the hatch computer in "Adrift."

- The numbers appear on the vial that Claire was injected with in the medical station in "Maternity Leave."

- The numbers appear on the blast door in the Swan station in "Lockdown."

- The numbers appear on LAPD police cars in "Two for the Road." [4]

As if this repeating series of numbers were not enough to drive *Lost* researchers into hyperdrive, lists of the occurrences of each number now dominate fan sites, with dozens of citations for the individual integers in the series of numbers. For instance, the number 42 shows up at least four times in "Exodus, Part 1":

- Ana Lucia sat in seat **42**F.

- Hurley's hotel room in Sydney was number 23**42**.

- Hurley's car had gone **42** km when it broke down on his way to the airport.

- There were **42** original survivors from the front section of the plane at the end of Season One in "Exodus, Part 1." [5]

There is even a Web site that lists the occurrences of numbers *outside* of the *Lost* numbers, ranging from 1 (the number of bullets left in the marshal's gun after Sawyer shoots the polar bear) to 156 million (the amount of money Hurley is worth when he crashes on the island). [6]

Number Theories

Much has been made of the meanings behind the numbers in *Lost*, but one of the most intriguing can be made for the location of the island itself: Latitude 4.815 and Longitude 162.342 (which together creates the string 4815162342) are the GPS coordinates that lead to a point in the Pacific Ocean on the trail from Australia to Los Angeles, California. Try out the coordinates yourself at mapquest.com and see where they lead. Maybe the numbers on the hatch are GPS coordinates rather than bad luck?

What Can Be Found in *Lost*?

Some have noted the parallels between the numbers in *Lost* and how numbers are used in special ways in various religions. For example, the number 108 is highly sacred to Buddhists, Hindus, and some Muslims. There are 108 stars of destiny, 108 beads on a *mala* (a string of beads used during meditation), 108 seats in the Nepalese parliament, 108 moves in many tai chi sequences, 108 sins in Tibetan Buddhism (that must be overcome to achieve nirvana), and it is the symbol of Siva in Hinduism and of *surat al-Kawthar* in the Qur'an.

...And Names

While names are a much smaller part of the *Lost* craze than the infamous string of numbers, there is a strange repetition of names that appears across multiple characters in *Lost*. Some examples include:

Brian: 1) The name of Walt's stepfather, 2) the name of Shannon's boyfriend in Australia.

Danielle: 1) Rousseau's first name, 2) the name of the girl who died during an operation performed by Christian Shephard when he was drunk.

Rutherford: 1) Shannon's last name, 2) the last name of

the SUV driver who died (we later discover that Shannon is the man's daughter).

Sarah: 1) Ana-Lucia's Australian alias name, 2) the name of Jack's wife.

Thomas: 1) The name of Claire's boyfriend, 2) the name of Kate's childhood friend.[7]

One religion that focuses heavily on the study of numbers is Kabbalah, a mystical religion with roots in Judaism. Kabbalists believe that their scripture (the Torah) is inspired not just in its obvious interpretations, but also in numerous hidden meanings. They believe that by interpreting and applying various numerical formulas, they can find hidden messages embedded in the Torah. Further, Kabbalists hold that this mystical system was revealed by God at the same time as the revelation of the Torah, and that each letter in the Torah has an underlying, secret significance.[8] Sound familiar? The same practice has been used in varying degrees by fans of *Lost* to discover the hidden meaning of the numbers that appear in various episodes of *Lost*.

The Strangest Numbers of All?

In "A Tale of Two Cities," Jack can be seen reaching for his beeper in a flashback. In a freeze frame, the beeper's time is shown as 7:15:23 a.m. Fifteen and 23 are both *Lost* numbers. It even includes words on the crossword puzzle under the beeper that contains significant words from the series, such as:

Prenatal: Relating to the special significance of the island's pregnancies.

Heroes: Such as Jack.

Heavy Drinker: Such as Jack's father.

We also see "raft," "necessary evils," and "essential facts." It is unclear how far this crossword puzzle was intended to be a clue, but simply shows that every scene of *Lost* is rich in multiple layers of meaning.

Numerology (the study of numbers) has also been used historically in ancient Babylonian religions, by Pythagoras in ancient Greece, in astrology, Gnosticism, Indian Vedas, the Chinese Circle of the Dead, and Egyptian religions. A special emphasis on numerical meaning is still found today in Chinese traditions and in astrology books.

Even the Bible has some numbers that are used in special ways. Jesus rose from the dead in three days, the universe was created in seven "days," and Moses led the Israelites in the wilderness for 40 years. All three numbers are used frequently throughout the Bible. But do such special uses of numbers determine our future, as taught in other religions?

According to the New Testament, the answer is a firm no. The apostle Paul wrote to the young church leader Timothy:

> As I urged you when I went into Macedonia, stay there in Ephesus so that you may command certain men not to teach false doctrines any longer *nor to devote themselves to myths and endless genealogies.* These promote controversies rather than God's work—which is by faith. The goal of this command is love, which comes from a pure heart and a good conscience and a sincere faith. Some have wandered away from these and turned to meaningless talk (1 Timothy 1:3-6).

What were these myths and genealogies? Ancient Ephesus promoted many alternative spiritual practices, and one of these likely included ancient numerology. Paul said Christians were to avoid such obsessions and to focus on God's work based on the goal of love. In other words, God has already revealed all we need to know within his written word.

God also invites us to come directly to him with our doubts and questions:

> *I have not spoken in secret,* from somewhere in a land of darkness; I have not said to Jacob's descendants, "Seek me in vain." I, the Lord, speak the truth; *I declare what is right.* Gather together and come; assemble, you fugitives from the

nations. Ignorant are those who carry about idols of wood, who pray to gods that cannot save. Declare what is to be, present it—let them take counsel together. Who foretold this long ago, who declared it from the distant past? Was it not I, the LORD? And there is no God apart from me, a righteous God and a Savior; there is none but me. Turn to me and be saved, all you ends of the earth; for I am God, and there is no other (Isaiah 45:19-22).

Here God shares that he is the one who created the universe and all that is in it. He alone knows all things and proves it by giving prophecies about the nations that were fulfilled with exact precision. He says that those who worship idols and pray to gods who cannot save them are foolish. Numerology can become a false god if it is given the belief it controls a person's destiny. Only God does that. To focus heavily on special numerical values or hidden meanings for further knowledge of the supernatural is unhealthy and taught against by the Bible.

Lost is great at keeping people guessing when it comes to numbers. But ultimately, as Hurley discovers, the numbers are not jinxed or cursed. He makes his own luck and uses a Volkswagen van from the island to rescue his friends. God calls us to use the resources he has provided in the Bible to seek the spiritual truth on issues related to the supernatural.

Lost Talk

- Do you think certain numbers have special significance? Why or why not?

- The Bible often uses certain numbers with a special significance. How is this different from how numbers are used in *Lost*?

- In what ways can an overemphasis on numerical meanings hinder how we live our lives?

LOST on Redemption

LOCKE: *Come here. I'm going to show you something. What do you suppose is in that cocoon, Charlie?*

CHARLIE: *I don't know, a butterfly, I guess?*

LOCKE: *No, it's much more beautiful than that. That's a moth cocoon. It's ironic, butterflies get all the attention, but moths...they spin silk, they're stronger, they're faster.*

CHARLIE: *That's wonderful, but...*

LOCKE: *You see this little hole? This moth's just about to emerge. It's in there right now, struggling, it's digging its way through the thick hide of the cocoon. Now, I could help it, take my knife, gently widen the opening, and the moth would be free. But it would be too weak to survive. The struggle is nature's way of strengthening it.*

—FROM "THE MOTH"

In "The Moth," Charlie continues to wrestle with his heroin addiction. In the process of helping Charlie, Locke tells him the story of the moth, explaining that the struggle to escape the cocoon is nature's way of strengthening the nocturnal insect. Locke sees Charlie as being like a moth and progressively convinces him that he is much stronger than he thinks. This metaphor serves as one of multiple examples of the concept of redemption in *Lost*.

In an interview with *Entertainment Weekly*, *Lost* cocreator Damon Lindelof shared that *Lost* is like other well-done character-focused shows in the sense that it is about people "searching for redemption in the face of their flaws and struggles."[1] In the series, redemption means to make a personal decision to live a more moral or spiritual life, a concept reflected in both the actions and stories told by characters in *Lost*. •

Addressing the Issue: "The struggle is nature's way of strengthening it."

In Season Two, it is Eko who becomes the storyteller among the survivors. During a scene with Michael in "Three Minutes," the two share the following conversation:

MICHAEL: *I hear you're a priest.*

EKO: *Yes.*

MICHAEL: *I guess you believe in hell, then.*

EKO: *For a brief time I served in a small parish in England. Every Sunday after Mass, I would see a young boy waiting at the back of the church. And then one day, the boy confessed to me that he had beaten his dog to death with a shovel. He said the dog had bitten his baby sister on the cheek and he needed to protect her. And he wanted to know whether he would go to hell for this. I told him that God would understand, that he would be forgiven, as long as he was sorry. But the boy did not care about forgiveness. He was only afraid that if he did go to hell, that dog would be there waiting for him.*

Why would Eko share such a story with Michael? Perhaps Eko

suspects that fear of punishment motivates Michael, just as it did the young boy.

Later in Season Two, we find Eko wrestling with redemption himself. Eko wonders if he is really good enough to be a priest, especially after impersonating one for so long. His violent past finally returns to haunt him in "The Cost of Living." In this episode, Eko claims he is not sorry for his past actions, and that he had done the best he could.

Other characters share their own ups and downs as they seek a new, different, and hopefully better life on the island. Hurley confronts the issue of food, his "friend" Dave, and his relationship with Libby. Charlie not only fights against his drug addiction, but shows his desire to be a respectable person who can care for Claire and Aaron and prove his worth to the other survivors.

Lost on Redemption

The following quotes reveal just a few of many other references to redemption and forgiveness in *Lost*:

In Personal Relationships

"I'm sorry Father. Please forgive me. I was…ashamed of you."

—Jin to his father, in "…In Translation"

"I can't say I understand what you're going through, but I know what it feels like when you lose family. I hope you can forgive me. I'm sorry."

—Locke to Shannon, in "The Greater Good"

"John, this is your last time to end this. Open the door, and I will forgive you."

—Eko, in "Live Together, Die Alone"

"I forgive you. When my husband returns, I will tell him I made terrible mistake, that it was not you…and he will release you."

—Amira, in "Enter 77"

With God

"Have you forgotten how you got that cross, brother...the day they took me? Is what I did that day a sin? Or is it forgiven because it was you that was saved?"
—Eko to Yemi, in "The 23rd Psalm"

"Perhaps we are, but God will forgive me, Eko."
—Yemi to Eko, in "The 23rd Psalm"

"Forgive me. Forgive me."
—Eko, in "The 23rd Psalm"

"To receive God's forgiveness you must be penitent for your sins."
—Eko, in "?"

"Lord, forgive me."
—Jack, in "Through the Looking Glass"

This redemptive idea of second chances is also important in the character of Ana-Lucia. Early on, she serves as an interrogator and leader for the survivors from the tail end of the airplane, portraying a hardened attitude that resembles her pre-island days with the LAPD. Later, she accidentally kills Shannon and becomes an outcast among the now-merged group of survivors.

In "Two for the Road," Ana-Lucia was strangled by Henry Gale (Ben) and has the opportunity to kill him. However, now she is unable, claiming she is "no longer that type of person." During her time on the island, she leaves her reckless and restless ways to become a more healthy and functioning member of the island community. However, her changed life, unfortunately, did not lead to a long life, as she soon dies at the hands of a murderer on the island.

What Can Be Found in *Lost*?

Lost reflects on the dilemma of broken relationships with family and friends and the need for forgiveness and restoration. We also find the theme of a broken relationship with God, including the distance we as humans often feel in relationship to the divine.

One book that analyzes redemption in *Lost* shares this:

> New lives require dedication and nurturing. Change is difficult to sustain, and even the best intentions are tough to maintain when people are stressed, overworked, and challenged. As these characters illustrate, redemption is an ongoing process that requires a daily desire to change for the better.[2]

From a human perspective, these words are right on target. But what about God's perspective? What does the Bible tell us about the important issues of redemption and second chances?

According to God's Word, all redemption—or salvation—begins with Jesus. He is the one *who redeems us.* Matthew 1:21 says, "She will give birth to a son, and you are to give him the name Jesus, because *he will save his people from their sins.*" Jesus is presented first and foremost as our redeemer, rescuer, and Savior (the one who saves us).

Second, we are told *what we are redeemed from:* "their sins." Let's face it—we all mess up on a regular basis. We might call our wrongdoings mistakes instead of sins, but both are the same thing to God. We need someone to change and redeem us because we are not perfect. Because of this fact of life, we need Jesus, according to the Bible, in order to change and live a life that is in line with God's original intentions and plans for us.

Third, the Bible communicates *what we are redeemed for:* to live out God's plan for our lives. Romans 12:2 encourages us by saying, "Don't copy the behavior and customs of this world, but *let God transform you into a new person* by changing the way you think. Then you will learn to know God's will for you, which is good and pleasing and perfect" (NLT). In *Lost*, characters often attempt to change in their own strength. Sometimes they succeed; sometimes they fail. However, God's strength is perfect (Psalm 18:32), making him able to bring about changes that we cannot.

That's the *who, what,* and *why* of redemption according to the Bible, and God's Word also tells us *when* redemption is available and *how* to receive it. The time to seek redemption, according to the book of Hebrews, is today. "Today, if you hear his voice, do not harden your hearts" (Hebrews 3:7-8). God's desire is for us to turn to him today so he can help us to change *now.*

The life of Jesus provides an excellent insight into how to receive redemption and the opportunity to start fresh. In Luke 19 we read about a tax collector named Zacchaeus. He was an outcast in his community because he worked for the Roman government that ruled over the Jewish people, and because tax collectors frequently collected more money than required so they could keep some for their own personal gain. Though others rejected Zacchaeus, Jesus didn't. He said he wanted to stop by Zacchaeus's home.

The crowd who heard Jesus' words to Zacchaeus immediately began their gossip. "He has gone to be the guest of a 'sinner'" (Luke 19:7). But later, we see that Jesus had a life-changing impact on Zacchaeus that day. After they met, Zacchaeus publicly committed to donating half of his possessions to the poor and to paying back four times the amount he had wrongly taken from taxpayers.

Jesus responded not to Zacchaeus's promised actions but to the attitude of the man's heart when he said, "Today *salvation* has come to this house, because this man, too, is a son of Abraham. For *the Son of Man came to seek and to save what was lost*" (19:9-10). Zacchaeus was redeemed by Jesus. Why? He experienced Jesus. Jesus came to seek and to redeem the lost.

═ Redeeming Our Relationships with Others ═

1. *Watch what you say:* "Sometimes it [our tongue] praises our Lord and Father, and sometimes it curses those who have been made in the image of God. And so blessing and cursing come pouring out of the same mouth. Surely, my brothers and sisters, this is not right!" (James 3:9-10 NLT).
2. *Confess failures:* "Confess your sins to each other

and pray for each other so that you may be healed"
(James 5:16 NLT).

3. *Encourage others:* "Let everything you say be good
   and helpful, so that your words will be an encouragement to those who hear them" (Ephesians 4:29
   NLT).

4. *Don't tell lies:* "Stop telling lies. Let us tell our
   neighbors the truth" (Ephesians 4:25 NLT).

5. *Don't be controlled by anger:* "Don't sin by letting
   anger control you" (Ephesians 4:25 NLT).

In *Lost*, there are many examples of redemption at the human level, but only Christ can radically transform the heart in an eternal way. To heal our broken relationship with God, we have to come to God on his terms. God already knows everything about us, good and bad, yet he still loves us. So why do we feel distant from God? Is it enough to just say, "I'm sorry"?

It's a good start, but it doesn't heal our broken relationship with God. It's like a man who kills his brother and says, "I'm sorry." The judge can accept the killer's apology in court, but the apology doesn't remove the punishment due as a result of the crime. God wants to free us from the punishment we deserve for our wrongs *and* provide a restored relationship with him.

This is where Jesus is so important. God sent Jesus to death on the cross to pay the punishment for our wrongs. Without Jesus, we can say we're sorry, yet we will still be alienated from God. But through a relationship with Christ, we can experience true forgiveness, have our sins washed away, and enjoy a personal relationship with God.

I (John) taped a television program with a young man who had placed his trust in Christ after making a living as a homosexual prostitute. A month after taping that program, this man died from AIDS. My friend Erwin Lutzer, a pastor, also knew this man. One day when we were recording a broadcast together, Erwin referred to this person, saying, "Think of two books. The first is called *The Life and Times of*

Roger [not the man's real name]. A second book is called *The Life and Times of Jesus Christ*. When you open the covers of *The Life and Times of Roger*, you see all the sins of Roger's life. There, for everyone to witness, are greed and lust. Roger had over 1100 sexual partners during his life, leaving a trail of lies, anger, and hurt toward many of the people around him. Yet when you open the cover of the second book, *The Life and Times of Jesus Christ*, you see all of Jesus' perfections and absolute purity.

"Now picture what happened the moment Roger placed his faith in Christ. God ripped the covers off both books and put the contents of *The Life and Times of Roger* between the pages of *The Life and Times of Jesus Christ*. After that, every time God opens *The Life and Times of Roger*, he sees only the perfect life of Christ."

What can be found in *Lost* is the *desire* to change. What can be found in Christ is the *power* to change. (If you would like to find out more about beginning your own relationship with Christ now, please turn now to "*Lost*...What to Do About It" before continuing to another chapter. We hope you, too, experience the wonderful redemption available only through Jesus.)

Lost Talk

- What is the most powerful example of redemption or a changed life you have seen on *Lost*?

- This chapter speaks of restoring broken relationships with other people and restoring the broken relationship with God. In what ways are these two types of redemption different? How are they similar?

- What are some of the reasons people give for putting off a relationship with Christ until another time? How can a person be encouraged to take action now rather than later?

LOST on Death

12

JACK: *What do you mean you won't put it on the plane?*

CHRISSY: *I'm sorry, Mr. Shephard, but our policy is that the body must have the proper documentation. There's just no latitude.*

JACK: *No latitude? No latitude?*

CHRISSY: *Without the proper documents…*

JACK: *Look, you can't do this to me. I'm ready to go now.*

CHRISSY: *Perhaps another carrier…*

JACK: *No! I want you to listen to me, okay? Because I'm asking you a favor, Chrissy. I'm standing in front of you in the same suit that I'm wearing to my father's funeral and I'm asking you a favor. In 16 hours I need to land at LAX, and I need that coffin to clear customs because there's going to be a hearse waiting there. And I need that hearse to take me and that coffin to a cemetery. Why? Chrissy, why can't I just bring him to a funeral home and make all the arrangements? Why can't I really take my time*

> with it? Because…because I need it to be done.
> I need it to be over. I just…I need to bury my
> father.
>
> —FROM "WHITE RABBIT"

One important and unavoidable issue that arises in *Lost* is death. And one of the most insightful looks into death is found not in the situations that arise in the plane crash itself, but in the flashback of Jack at the airport discussing the transportation of his father's corpse.

Addressing the Issue: "I need it to be over."

Many have noted that Jack Shephard feels the need to save or fix everyone. When he loses a patient, he struggles to accept what happened. It becomes a very personal issue. Upon the deaths of fellow survivors, he has found himself speechless or feeling helpless. At Boone's funeral in "Exodus," Jack says nothing. Sayid becomes the leader who steps forward to speak words of encouragement. Later, we find Jack at Shannon's funeral, and Sayid is the one who now cannot speak the words he holds inside. In a bit of contrast, Jack still remains speechless, yet helps by beginning the ritual of tossing dirt into the grave.

Yet Jack takes complete control of one burial in "Whatever the Case May Be." When the marshal dies, Jack draws on some type of religious background to bury the man and place a cross at the grave. Perhaps Jack is driven by the guilt he feels from not being able to save him. Kate asks, "So why didn't you put him with the others when you burned the fuselage?"

Jack responds, "Because I needed to bury him."

═══ Where Are the Bodies Going? ═══

Bodies of dead people on the island seem to keep disappearing. The living survivors who had connections with the dead people later have visions of them alive. For example, Jack's father, Christian, is missing from his coffin. Jack then sees his father alive on the beach and in the jungle. Even stranger (if that's possible) is what happens to Eko's brother, Yemi. Eko is stunned to discover his brother's dead body on the crashed Beechcraft plane, but when he returns to the crash site, Yemi's body is missing! Hurley even jokes that Ethan will return from the dead and chase the castaways through the jungle. This strange pattern of disappearances and visions will continue to haunt the minds of *Lost* fans possibly all the way to the end of the series.

Repeatedly we find that the characters of *Lost* struggle to find ways to cope with the magnitude of and the number of deaths in their midst. Charlie, for example, feels obligated to bury Ethan, though he had shot him with no remorse. A growing cemetery near the beach continues to stand as a reminder of the stark reality that death could claim any one of the survivors at any time.

The Others hold their own unique brand of funeral ceremonies, including traditions that are reminiscent of those observed by the Vikings or those in the Lord of the Rings trilogy. The ritual of placing a dead body on a raft, setting it on fire, and then watching it drift away upon the ocean stands in stark contrast with the more informal burials of the Oceanic survivors. In "The Cost of Living," the Others attend their funeral ceremonies dressed completely in white, which is reminiscent of more formal Eastern religious traditions.

=== **Did You Know...** ===

...that up through Season Three, 72 people have died on the island or during flashbacks/flash forwards on *Lost?*[1]

The castaways on *Lost* utilize several different death and funeral traditions. Those without a belief system are shown as unable to cope or fight to deal with each crisis. While having faith doesn't protect those with belief systems from death or its associated problems, those who hold to a set of spiritual principles (such as Eko, Rose, Desmond, or Charlie) appear to cope best with the losses of human life.

Lost on Death

"It was a distress call from a French woman. She said that the others were dead, something had killed them all. She was alone on the island. It's been playing for sixteen years, Jack. I wanted to tell you."

—Kate, in "Tabula Rasa"

"Do you do this back home, too, steal from the dead?"

—Jack to Sawyer, in "Tabula Rasa"

"You know, your life would be so much easier if you just had the manifest. We crossed out all the names of the dead after we burned the fuselage, so it should be a full roster of the rest of us."

—Boone, in "Raised by Another"

"Don't knock the obits…the nicest part of the paper. No one ever says anything mean about people once they're dead."

—Helen, in "Lockdown"

"They found the plane. There were no survivors. They were all dead."

—Naomi, in "D.O.C."

What Can Be Found in *Lost*?

What can we learn from *Lost* on the issue of death? First, *Lost* provides several clear examples that inevitably, everyone will die. Death is unavoidable. But why? The Bible gives the answer in Genesis 3. Adam and Eve were told by God that if they ate from the forbidden tree, they would die. When they disobeyed God, they died spiritually—their relationship with God was broken and later, they died physically. God told them, "By the sweat of your brow you will eat your food until you return to the ground, since from it you were taken; for dust you are and to dust you will return" (Genesis 3:19).

Adam and Eve's rebellion against God and resulting deaths set a pattern for every human being who has followed.

Lost also shows numerous occasions in which the castaways must deal with the deaths of those around them, including loved ones or friends. Often the island survivors are at a loss regarding how to respond. While death is never easy for anyone, the Bible offers the hope of eternal life for those who have personal faith in Christ. As we will discuss in the next chapter ("*Lost* on the Afterlife"), rather than feeling only sorrow and despair, Christians can also experience a hope for the future because of what happens in the afterlife.

Death Matters

"It is hard to have patience with people who say 'There is no death' or 'Death doesn't matter.' There is death. And whatever is matters. And whatever happens has consequences, and it and they are irrevocable and irreversible. You might as well say that birth doesn't matter."

—C.S. Lewis[2]

A striking example of hope in the midst of death stood out to me when I (John) watched an interview with Jackie Kennedy's son after his mother's death. The son said he was sad at the loss of his mother, but he looked forward to the day when he would see her again in heaven. I appreciated his comment, and was surprised by the response from some of the reporters. Repeatedly they asked Jackie's son if he really believed that heaven was a real place and whether he really thought he would see his mother there. They questioned whether heaven is a real place.

Is heaven a real place? If it is real, everyone wants to go there. How can we know for sure? The Bible tells us, "I write these things to you who believe in the name of the Son of God *so that you may know that you have eternal life*" (1 John 5:13). If the Bible is true, then heaven is a real place, and we can know whether we will be there. (We'll talk more about this in the next chapter.)

Personally, I (Dillon) struggled when my father died seven years ago (at the time of this writing). He was only 49 years old, and I had seen him just four days before he passed away. Just as the characters on *Lost* have grieved for their loved ones and friends, I grieved the fact that I would no longer share time with my dad here in this life. Yet as followers of Christ, my father and I share a hope based on God's Word—a hope that tells us that this life is not all there is. In the midst of my sorrow, I could look forward to a future time when I will be reunited with my father in the presence of God in heaven.

While we see hints of this type of belief in episodes of *Lost*, there is more doubt about death than understanding. Much of this doubt arises from the views and beliefs various characters have regarding the afterlife—a theme we will explore in our next chapter.

Lost Talk

- Why is it difficult for most people to talk about death?

- Everyone will die eventually. How can we best prepare ourselves for this reality?

- Why do you think people don't usually say negative things about someone who has just died?

LOST on the Afterlife

DESMOND:	*I'm going to blow the dam, John. I'm sorry for whatever happened that made you stop believing. But it's all real…and now I've got to go and make it all go away.*
LOCKE:	*Wait. Desmond!*
DESMOND:	*I'll see you in another life, brother.*
PA SYSTEM:	*System failure. System failure. System failure…*

—FROM "LIVE TOGETHER, DIE ALONE"

In "Live Together, Die Alone," we find Desmond holding an emergency key, prepared to implode the Swan station to end the disaster that is taking place in the hatch. Before Desmond's final descent, he leaves Locke with the parting words, "I'll see you in another life, brother."

Ironically, this comment that seems to affirm reincarnation comes from the lips of a man who was a former monk. As a monk, Desmond would have been trained in the Catholic perspectives of heaven, hell, and purgatory.

Anthony Cooper, when in captivity on the island, believes he is in hell, whereas Rose speaks to her "heavenly Father." Then there are skeptics such as Jack and Sawyer, who wonder if there is anything after this life.

So what can we learn about the afterlife in *Lost?* Are we destined to return in numerous life cycles, is the island hell itself, or do some of the afterlife themes of *Lost* direct us toward what God says really will happen to us beyond this life?

Addressing the Issue: "I'll see you in another life, brother."

Some have observed that one of the dominant religious perspectives in *Lost* is Buddhism. On the theme of the afterlife, this is clearly the case. Buddhism believes in multiple reincarnations, which is in line with what we hear from the lips of Desmond. A very visual example is also found in the death of Boone during "Do No Harm." Boone was the first major character to die on the island. His death scene is intercut with scenes of the birth of Claire's baby. As Jack cries over Boone's body, Claire's face radiates with tears of joy. The cycle of life continues, with birth and death in close connection.

A look at other references to the afterlife in *Lost* reveals other religious perspectives in addition to Buddhism.

════ *Lost* on the Afterlife ════

- Rose prays to God in heaven with Charlie in "Whatever the Case May Be."

- Sayid reads the back of Nadia's picture in "Solitary," which says, "You'll find me in the next life if not in this one."

- Both Locke (in "The Whole Truth") and Desmond (in "Man of Science, Man of Faith") mention the devil.

- Locke tells a story about how his foster mother believed his foster sister had come back to life as a golden retriever in "Outlaws."

- Sawyer is convinced that Frank Druckett's spirit inhabits the body of a boar in "Outlaws."

- Anthony looks to Locke before his kidney surgery and says, "See you on the other side, son" in "Deus ex Machina."

- Carmen mentions Jesus coming down from heaven in "Everybody Hates Hugo."

- Claire thinks baptism can get her and Aaron to heaven in "Fire + Water."

- Desmond tells Jack, "See you in another life, yeah?" in "Man of Science, Man of Faith."

- Hurley's "friend" Dave tells him he will see him in another life before jumping over a cliff in "Dave."

- Charlotte came back to life with a near-death story about Yemi in "?".

- Desmond tells Locke, "I'll see you in another life, brother" in "Live Together, Die Alone."

- Anthony tells Sawyer he thinks he is in hell when tied up inside the Black Rock in "The Brig."

- Charlie crosses himself before drowning, looking forward to heaven in "Through the Looking Glass."

We find references to Protestant and Catholic views of heaven, hell, purgatory, and near-death experiences. What is clear is that there is no clear consensus among the survivors regarding what happens after a person dies. Though all of the castaways wish for the departed to rest in peace, they hold to different views regarding if and how this will happen.

In *Lost*, there is also much attention placed on the concept of rebirth. All the survivors experience a type of rebirth when they crash on the island. And the theme of rebirth surfaces elsewhere. For example, the episode "Tabula Rasa" (a phrase meaning "clean slate" from the writings of philosopher John Locke) includes an emphasis on a new start.

Ray tells Kate in one flashback, "Everyone deserves a fresh start." Jack echoes these words later in the episode when he says, "We should all be able to start over."

Locke himself gets in on the rebirth discussion when he confronts Shannon about her attitude in "…In Translation." He says, "Everyone gets a new life on this island, Shannon. Maybe it's time you start yours." In "House of the Rising Sun," Charlie starts over (eventually) by kicking his heroin addiction and seeking to become a reliable friend and companion to Claire.

It is Kate, however, who takes the concept of a rebirth or fresh start most seriously. She hides her past as a convict and even steals another person's ID so she can start with a new identity once saved on the raft. However, over time, her past comes back both to reveal "What Kate Did" (one entire episode) as well as to help the other castaways through some of her unique skills.

Rebirth and reincarnation are often associated in religious tradition. These themes can be found everywhere from the concept of being "born again" in Christianity to the Muslim concept of prescribed rites as part of spiritual rebirth to the literal reincarnation philosophies of Eastern religions, paganism, and Wicca. But when it comes to the afterlife (especially our own), how can we know which view is true?

══════ The Philosophers of *Lost* ══════

Did you know that many of the character names in *Lost* are the same as those of famous philosophers and thinkers? These connections might not be tied to the idea of reincarnation, but it is interesting how the show's characters sometimes resemble the thinkers they are named after. They include Richard Alpert, Mikhail Bakunin, Edmund Burke, Boone Carlyle (Thomas Carlyle), Anthony Cooper, Desmond David Hume, John Locke, and Jean-Jacques Rousseau (Danielle).[1]

What Can Be Found in *Lost*?

Lost constantly portrays the castaways dealing with issues of life and death and death's implications. Sayid struggles with the death of Shannon after Shannon has just dealt with the loss of Boone. Many of these characters are young and have lived without much thought of what might happen to them after they die. Among the characters we see references to heaven, hell, purgatory, annihilation (ceasing to exist), and reincarnation. These relate to the common views of the afterlife in our world today, which include:

Annihilation	Life ends at physical death.
Reincarnation	Life repeats in various forms.
Purgatory	A "middle ground" between heaven and hell, where many go for a temporary cleansing before entering heaven.
Universalism	Everyone goes to heaven.
Works-based Afterlife	Afterlife will be determined by how many good deeds a person has done.
Biblical Christianity	Those who have trusted in Jesus by faith go to heaven; those who have not go to hell. Rejects the other five views.

While *Lost* covers all the above options, it is in the Bible that we find the most accurate information about the afterlife. The book of Hebrews speaks of physical death, stating, "Man is destined to die once, and after that to face judgment" (9:27). Job, in the book of the Bible that bears his name, wrote, "Naked I came from my mother's womb, and naked I will depart" (Job 1:21). King Solomon further noted that there is a time to be born and a time to die (Ecclesiastes 3:2). According to the Bible, then, there is no such thing as reincarnation.

If our body dies only once, then what happens after we die? So far, we have noted that at death, we receive a judgment (Hebrews 9:27). This indicates that we do not cease to exist, but rather, that we spiritually exist in the afterlife in some way (our soul or spirit). In the Bible, two destinies are mentioned: heaven or hell. And we are given a glimpse into both places through the teachings of Jesus. In Luke 16:19-31, we find this account:

> There was a rich man who was dressed in purple and fine linen and lived in luxury every day. At his gate was laid a beggar named Lazarus, covered with sores and longing to eat what fell from the rich man's table. Even the dogs came and licked his sores.

> The time came when the beggar died and the angels carried him to Abraham's side. The rich man also died and was buried. In hell, where he was in torment, he looked up and saw Abraham far away, with Lazarus by his side. So he called to him, "Father Abraham, have pity on me and send Lazarus to dip the tip of his finger in water and cool my tongue, because I am in agony in this fire."

> But Abraham replied, "Son, remember that in your lifetime you received your good things, while Lazarus received bad things, but now he is comforted here and you are in agony. And besides all this, between us and you a great chasm has been fixed, so that those who want to go from here to you cannot, nor can anyone cross over from there to us."

> He answered, "Then I beg you, father, send Lazarus to my father's house, for I have five brothers. Let him warn them, so that they will not also come to this place of torment."

> Abraham replied, "They have Moses and the Prophets; let them listen to them."

> "No, father Abraham," he said, "but if someone from the dead goes to them, they will repent."

> He said to him, "If they do not listen to Moses and the Prophets, they will not be convinced even if someone rises from the dead."

Notice how these verses describe what Lazarus and the rich man experienced:

Lazarus	Rich man
With Abraham (verse 22)	In torment (verses 23-28)
Comforted (verse 25)	In agony (verses 24-25)
Experienced the sights of heaven	He could talk, feel pain, remember the past, and make requests

Also, look at how much time lapsed between their physical deaths, and when Lazarus entered heaven and the rich man entered hell. They closed their eyes in this life and opened them in the next. The transition was described as instantaneous.

Furthermore, notice what we are told about the separation between heaven and hell: "Between us and you a great chasm has been fixed, so that those who want to go from here to you cannot, nor can anyone cross over from there to us" (verse 26). This statement clearly erases purgatory as an afterlife option (though it is still taught in Roman Catholic theology).

Lost certainly deals with issues of the afterlife head-on, offering opportunities to investigate this matter further, either personally or with others. Claire wonders what will happen to Aaron if he dies and whether she will be with him. She concludes that baptism is necessary. Likewise, the (literally!) explosive death of Arzt causes shock and a moment for the survivors to consider their own mortality in "Exodus." (Who can forget Hurley's famous line, "You've got some Arzt on you"?) While we often prefer not to think about or discuss what will happen to us when we die, *Lost* forces us to grapple with this all-important area of life, one that we will develop further in the final chapter of this book.

Before ending this chapter, we want to share with you the words of the only person to ever die and physically come back to life by his own power—Jesus Christ. His resurrection from the dead gives him the authority—over all religions and religious leaders—to speak on this topic. The actual phrase "eternal life" is used 14 times in the book of John in the Bible, many times in connection with Jesus Christ, emphasizing eternity with Christ as God's desire for our lives.

Eternal Life According to John's Gospel

#		
1.	"...that everyone who believes in him may have *eternal life.*"	3:15
2.	"...whoever believes in him shall not perish but have *eternal life.*"	3:16
3.	"Whoever believes in the Son has *eternal life...*"	3:36
4.	"The water I give him will become in him a spring of water welling up to *eternal life.*"	4:14
5.	"...even now he harvests the crop for *eternal life...*"	4:36
6.	"You diligently study the Scriptures because you think that by them you possess *eternal life.* These are the Scriptures that testify about me, yet you refuse to come to me to have life."	5:39-40
7.	"Do not work for food that spoils, but for food that endures to *eternal life,* which the Son of Man will give you."	6:27
8.	"Everyone who looks to the Son and believes in him shall have *eternal life...*"	6:40
9.	"Whoever eats my flesh and drinks my blood has *eternal life,* and I will raise him up at the last day."	6:54
10.	"Lord, to whom shall we go? You have the words of *eternal life.*"	6:68
11.	"I give them *eternal life,* and they shall never perish..."	10:28
12.	"The man who loves his life will lose it, while the man who hates his life in this world will keep it for *eternal life.*"	12:25
13.	"For I did not speak of my own accord, but the Father who sent me commanded me what to say and how to say it. I know that his command leads to *eternal life.*"	12:49-50
14.	"For you granted him authority over all people that he might give *eternal life* to all those you have given him."	17:2

Is there any reason you would not desire this eternal life for yourself right now? If you want to find out more about what it means to make this decision, please turn to the section *"Lost...*What to Do About It" (page 145) before moving on to the next chapter.

Lost Talk

- How important is it to know what we believe regarding the afterlife? Why do you believe this way?

- What view of the afterlife makes the most sense to you? What information helped you arrive at this decision?

- Why do you think discussions about the afterlife are almost always in connection with a religion? How does a person's religious beliefs help determine his or her views about the afterlife?

PART TWO:
The Theories of *Lost*

Researching the World of **LOST**

Researching the world of *Lost* is more than just a pastime for many fans. With the explosion in Internet and video technology combined with high personal interest, fan research and speculation has reached a level unparalleled by any previous show of only three seasons. As a result, after Season Three, *Lost* was awarded by *TV Guide* with a number-five ranking in a list of the top cult television shows (cult in the sense of having a serious fan base and following).[1] As we delve into the facets of *Lost* research, we find that there are two major components to discuss: the researchers, and the research itself.

The Researchers: The *Lost*ologists

Creating a television series that attracts the kind of fan base *Lost* enjoys is no small accomplishment. *Lost* not only has a large number of fans, the show has achieved cult-level interest. *Lost* fans, also known as Losties, have created a written, audio, and video culture online unlike that of any previous television show. While many factors have made this possible, the following four things have played major roles in fueling this interest.

Lostpedia.com and the Wiki Phenomenon

Lostpedia.com is simply the *Lost* version of Wikipedia.com. Any registered user can add to, subtract from, or edit entries, articles, and photographs related to a wide variety of *Lost* topics. Losties also engage in debates that discuss the mysterious appearance of Kate's horse, the identification of the Hanso Foundation, and the four-toed statue. This keeps Losties busy between episodes and during the long hiatus between each season.

As of the time of this writing, 3222 articles are logged within the Web site's files. According to the site itself, over 80 million page hits have been made to date, making it one of the most-visited wiki sites on the Web outside of Wikipedia.com. Of those who have visited, more than 19,500 are registered users who have contributed information. The group is currently led by nine sysops (system operators) who live in various locations across the United States, the United Kingdom, and Ireland.

Lost on Campus

As *Lost*'s popularity has grown, so has the interest of academic researchers at the college and professional levels. The creation of the Society for the Study of *Lost* is one striking example of people who have come together to discuss *Lost*. This society publishes an online peer-reviewed journal and detailed scholarly essays on themes within the episodes of *Lost*.

In addition, *Lost* has been featured in panels of other scholarly groups such as the Popular Culture Association and at the Hawaiian International Conference on the Arts and Humanities.[2]

Lost Gaming

For the many video- and computer-game-loving *Lost* fans, options include mobile games, an iPod game, a video game (still in development), and the *Lost* Experience. The *Lost* Experience was by far the most popular experiment, offering an online gaming experience. This

ARG (alternate reality game) is "a multimedia treasure hunt that makes use of e-mail messages, phone calls, commercials, billboards and fake websites that are made to seem real."[3] It was even created by the show's writers themselves. According to Lostpedia.com:

> *The* Lost *Experience* was internet-based and featured a parallel story line that was not part of the TV show. There were no winning prizes, but the *Experience* claimed to offer clues that could unlock some of the island's many secrets. It included the introduction of new characters and the mysterious Hanso Foundation. Clues were varied by continent, so participants would benefit from coordinating their information via the internet. ABC said the game was designed to appeal to both fans and people unfamiliar with *Lost*.[4]

Though down for now, many of the fans and players of *The* Lost *Experience* are hoping for its eventual return.

Lost Fan Conventions and Parties

In June 2004, Touchstone Pictures and ABC hired Creation Entertainment, famous for their fan development work for *The X-Files*, *Star Trek*, and *Xena*, to host a series of *Lost* conventions. At the first convention the start-up of *Lost* magazine was announced, memorabilia was sold, and appearances were made by some members of the cast. The *Lost* craze had resulted in conventions outside the United States as well, especially in the United Kingdom.[5] On a more local level, many clubs and groups of friends joined together for season premiere or season finale parties.

The Results: Technology + Motivation = Endless Speculation

The research done by fans to investigate various aspects of *Lost* has utilized many newer media and fringe media technologies of which many people are unaware. And there are some notable aspects of *Lost*-mania worthy of mention, too.

Freeze-frame Technology Yields Hidden Clues

Freeze-frame technology (both on television and computers) has been used heavily by *Lost* researchers. One Web site that actively resorts to this technology is is Sledgeweb's *Lost* (lost.cubit.net), which includes an in-depth section called "investigations."

These investigations, of which there are 278 at the time of this writing, include copies of freeze-frame screen-shot photographs of significant scenes. This allows users to view and post their observations (in fact, this book's investigation of Eko's Jesus Stick was based on photos from this site). Topics include everything from close-ups of Hurley's flight information to enlargements of Desmond's letter in Season Two to an analysis of Ben's diary entry from Season Three. Some of the more popular topics, such as the smoke monster, have been viewed nearly 10,000 times.

Based on many clues that can be found in such photos, numerous observations have been catalogued on this and other Web sites for the purpose of figuring out what might happen next in *Lost*. *Lost* has probably had more screenshots taken of its various episodes than any other television show in history.

Time-shift Television

Time shifting is the recording or downloading of a program to be watched at a different time. First popularized by TiVo, the practice of recording favorite programs for later usage is now a household norm for many Americans. The following options are used by many *Lost* viewers:

- DVR/TiVo: DVRs are digital video recording devices that are now common as part of cable television or satellite television packages. They allow users to save programs and watch them later. It's like having a digital VCR to record a program while away from home. An advanced way of using this technology is to later watch the program on one's computer in order to pause, zoom in, take screen shots, and record audio segments for analysis.

- iTunes: iTunes began selling *Lost* as a download that could be purchased within 24 hours of the television airing of each episode. *Lost* has remained one of the most downloaded programs on iTunes since its start.

- ABC Online: Season Three of *Lost* was also available to high-speed Internet users, along with viewer commercials, at abc.com.

While some have argued that *Lost* has lost some viewers over the past season, these arguments are based on Neilson ratings that do not take into account many of the above technologies. Since the 18- to 49-year-old segment is *Lost*'s largest audience, it makes sense that *Lost* is considered one of the most highly time-shifted shows."[6]

Fan Web Sites, Blogs, and Forums

One of the more popular fan forums is lost-media.com, which has been in operation since March 2004. It currently includes over 12,000 subscribers and a total of over 170 million page views. Another popular fan Web site and forum is Sledgeweb's *Lost*, which has been active since the beginning of the series. Its forum statistics as of this writing note that it includes more than 285,000 posts on 8700 topics related to *Lost*. It has hosted as many as 968 users at one time! Other popular forums include:[7]

- Losthatch.com: My (Dillon's) personal favorite, which includes a searchable database of the entire *Lost* series of transcripts. Site stats include more than 49 million hits and 8.5 million unique visitors.

- TheFuselage.com: The official forum for the series, it boasts more than 1.5 million posts and a stunning 57,000 members.

- Lostvideo.net: Includes more than 3400 videos created by fans of *Lost*.

- Lost-forum.com: Includes more than 1.3 million posts with nearly 87,000 members.

- Longlostlist.net: The forum section of longlostlist .com, consisting of more than 5900 articles.

- Thelostnumbers.blogspot.com: This site focuses solely on the numbers in *Lost*, and has received more than 1.3 million hits in just over two years.

- Lostfanatics.forumup.org: This forum site includes more than 36,822 articles about various aspects of *Lost*.

These numbers reveal the tremendous interest in the series, but one *Lost*ologist site tops them all. TheLostWorldBook.com includes a section called "Glossary" that is more of a key-word-coded dictionary for every bit of trivia imaginable about *Lost*. Even times such as "8:15 a.m." are included, with the explanation "The time of Adam Rutherford's death ('Man of Science, Man of Faith') are the same numbers as Oceanic Flight 815."

Time Line Mania

Another aspect of *Lost*mania is the meticulous work by some fans who attempt to piece together a chronological time line of the series. While this process originally began as an effort to track down dates within *Lost*, the practice has now expanded to include pre- and post-crash dates as well.

The earliest pre-crash dates include references from the date of the Black Rock's shipwreck in 1881 to the exact date April 9, 2007, which marks the latest point in the flash-forward shown in the Season Three finale, "Through the Looking Glass." This 2007 date appeared on the copy of the *Los Angeles Times* held by Jack. Based on the chronology pieced together by various sources, the information points to Season Three ending on December 23, 2004 (in island time). This indicates that Season Four will open with an episode that will take the castaways through the Christmas holiday and New Year's.[8]

The Numbers

While freeze-frame analysis and time line compilation have become part of the norm in *Lost* fandom, no facet of the series has drawn as much attention as the eerie series of numbers 4-8-15-16-23-42. While exact counts vary, this series of numbers together has appeared at least 18 times. In addition, various combinations of the numbers have appeared in nearly every numerical reference in the series, ranging from Leonard Simms playing Connect 4 in "Numbers," Oceanic Flight 815 (two of the numbers), to the flight leaving from Gate 23. The fan Web site 4815162342.com provides the most comprehensive treatment of the number series, whether in sequence, in other combinations, or individually. This site, along with others, has also taken this number hunting far beyond the original sequence to include count of every number used in *Lost* (see the chapter "*Lost* on Numbers" for more on this).

The "Other" Others

Then there are the "other" Others, those who could be called the true *Lost*ologists. There are a few diehard loyalists who not only participate in the fan culture, but lead it. These might include those who coordinate various fan Web sites and forums, but also include those analyzing the most seemingly impossible details or theories. This type of activity could include creating translations of the Korean conversations between Jin and Sun or of Rousseau's distress transmission.

A perfect example of this type of fringe activity includes research of what has become known as the Whispers. The Whispers come from an unknown frequency when characters are in peril or other moments of tension. According to those who have researched this material, these are not random noises, but actual speech that can be decoded with the proper audio technologies. The first account of the Whispers occurred in "Solitary" (the ninth episode of Season One), in which Sayid is captured by Rousseau in the jungle. According to Lostpedia.com, the following can be decoded:

MALE Voice:	*"Just let him get out of here."*
MALE Voice:	*"He's seen too much already."*
MALE Voice:	*"What if he tells?"*
FEMALE Voice:	*"Could just speak to him…"*
MALE Voice:	*"No."*

At least one Web site is devoted exclusively to decoding the Whispers (lostwhispering.blogspot.com). According to the site, some whispers can easily be heard by slowing down the audio, while others can be picked up using the right or left audio channel on a stereo system. Some of the hidden whispers require the use of audio software to separate the overlaying voices in order to decode them. In total, at least 12 accounts of the Whispers have been discovered to date.

Some fans have even gone so far as to attempt to discover hidden messages by playing particular audio segments backwards. There has been some speculation regarding the reverse audio of the Trippy movie in "Not in Portland"[9] and Walt's dialogue with Shannon in "Abandoned" and in "Man of Science, Man of Faith."[10]

Spectators of Speculation

What are we to think about all the fan activity surrounding *Lost?* Are these practices merely entertainment, or is there a risk of going to the point of unhealthy obsession? In the Bible, the apostle Paul makes two comments that can be taken into consideration here.

First, those who are followers of Christ are told to test everything. "Test everything. Hold on to the good. Avoid every kind of evil" (1 Thessalonians 5:21-22). This could certainly include the media we consume, whether television, radio, Internet, music, video games, or other forms of entertainment. When it comes to a show such as *Lost,* there is no harm in investigating the meanings of the happenings in the episodes, especially their spiritual implications, in order to better understand the show's messages and impact on our culture.

But Paul also gave another guideline worth paying attention to. He wrote to his young protégé Timothy and said,

> …remain on at Ephesus so that you may instruct certain men not to teach strange doctrines, nor to pay attention to myths and endless genealogies, which give rise to mere speculation rather than furthering the administration of God which is by faith.
>
> But the goal of our instruction is love from a pure heart and a good conscience and a sincere faith. For some men, straying from these things, have turned aside to fruitless discussion (1 Timothy 1:3-6 NASB).

In Timothy's situation in Ephesus (modern-day Turkey), there were some people who focused on extreme details of the Jewish law and others who participated in the pagan religious ideas and activities of Artemis (the goddess Diana). Those under Timothy's care had to be warned not to participate in the myths, endless genealogies, and ongoing speculations that promoted controversy rather than true faith. Why? Because the goal of the Christian is not controversy; it's love (verse 6).

So how do these biblical principles apply to *Lost*? According to the Bible, those who are Christians should take up the principle to test or consider the implications of what we allow into our lives. Is our participation good, or does it consume us? Our overarching goal must always be love from a pure heart, good conscience, and sincere faith. In doing so, we can help avoid becoming involved in things to the point that they hinder us from living out God's will for our lives.

Lost Talk

- Why do you think people like to research the clues and details of *Lost*?

- What are some of the positive things that can come from researching *Lost?* What are some of the negative?

- At what point do you think researching *Lost* (or any other show) could become unhealthy? Why do you feel this is the case?

Researching the (Many) Theories of LOST

15

An analysis of the theories precipitated by *Lost* could fill a book by itself! In fact, The Fuselage.com forum even includes a group called Q.U.E.S.T.: QUesting for Every Single Theory. Many of the theories circulating in fandom fall into similar categories, and the most comprehensive list available on the major theories may be the one on the *Lost* Wiki Web site at abc.com. This chapter will evaluate the strengths and weaknesses of ten of these major theories, and offer some comments about the theories of *Lost*.

Investigating the Theories

The top theories at ABC's site and compiled from other sources fall into seven categories. Some make more sense than others, and we will touch on each to better understand the thinking that takes place among the fans of *Lost*.

Theory #1: The Island Is Purgatory

In this popular theory, everyone on the island is actually dead after the plane crash, just as Naomi suggested in Season Three. Their actions on the island, according to this theory, will determine whether they ultimately end up in heaven or hell.

Please note that this theory is based on what fans think the show is about, not a biblical analysis of purgatory (see the chapter "*Lost* on the Afterlife"). Support for this theory comes from the idea that everyone on the island has a serious set of issues, and that the island itself seems to be working as a type of group therapy. Some have even noted that the name Gary Troup, the author of the *Lost* spinoff novel *Bad Twin*, is an anagram for purgatory (GARYTROUP=PURGATORY?).

However, even J.J. Abrams himself has dismissed this popular theory, stating that "it's not what it is, but it works as a metaphor for the show."[1] Physically, at least one character, Richard, is able to go on and off the island, meaning that not all the people on the island are limited to the island, as would be the case in purgatory.

Theory #2: It's the Future Affecting the Past

The idea behind this theory is that a major disaster has happened in the future and that somehow those in the future have alerted some people in the past about the disaster in order to help prevent it. A definite sci-fi scenario, it appeals to those who enjoy the concept of time-travel stories. The only evidence for this, however, seems to be the emphasis on Desmond's flashes (seemingly both past and future) and the use of a flash-forward in the Season Three finale.

The theory seems to miss out on major aspects of the show, especially the spiritual questions. In addition, it does not fit the scientific aspects involving the polar bears and animal experiments, nor does it provide any information to help identify or explain the smoke monster that keeps popping up along the way.

Theory #3: The Alien Theory

Are the castaways no longer on planet Earth? As the ABC wiki entry for this theory states, this would explain the monster and the other strange activities on the island. But does the fact there are some unexplained mysteries on the island necessarily mean the creators have alien abduction in mind?

According to co-creator Lindelof's comments on SciFiWire.com, the answer is a definite no. There are no spaceships, no aliens (that we know of so far), and there has been no time travel to date.

Theory #4: It's All in Someone's Mind

Polar bears, a smoke monster, an underground bunker on a deserted island—who wouldn't think it was all made up? While the show is fictional, the theory that the show's intent is that the series is within the mind of someone makes little sense for the show's creators. This *Matrix*-like perspective resembles the Buddhist mind-set that claims that reality is an illusion. But the problem is that there is no evidence that supports this theory. It is simply an easy way out of explaining the many mysteries in the series.

Theory #5: It's All a Government Experiment

Is the government behind the castaways' fate? This theory may have been more plausible early in the series, but by the latter part of Season Two we learn that the plane crashed due to an electromagnetic surge because a button was not pressed in time. This makes it highly unlikely any kind of government interference took place for the purpose of conducting an experiment.

Theory #6: Everything Happens for a Reason

Did the island choose each of the survivors for a reason? This theory works only if you believe the writers of the show planned for the island to be in control of what happens in the series. While possible, this is highly unlikely. Fate is a major part of the show, but is not the only theme at play. The emphasis on science (with the Others) in Season Three suggests that there may be more at work than destiny and fate, even if that is part of the end theory in *Lost*.

Theory #7: It's About the Chosen One

This theory believes that the island or someone on the island wanted only one passenger on Flight 815 (such as Walt or the unborn Aaron) and arranged for the flight to crash. However, Season Two revealed that the reason for the crash was not prearranged. Consequently, this theory does not hold much credibility. The fact the Others wanted the children and pregnant women from the crash seems to be more about their island science experiments rather than any kind of possible spiritual motivation for a chosen person.

Theory #8: The *Truman Show* Theory

In the *Truman Show* film, the character finds out that his entire life has been part of a staged show. While this matches the snow globe idea once mentioned by Desmond, how does this explain the deaths on the island? Also, unlike viewers of the *Truman Show*, the viewers of *Lost* are unaware of another group of outside observers watching their steps.

Theory #9: It's a Time Machine

Yes, some people really believe Flight 815 flew through a time-space portal of some sort and ended up lost somewhere in the past or future. This theory, however, seemed to lose its strength later in the series. By the time "The Glass Ballerina" aired in Season Three, we find Ben talking to Jack about current events, including the Red Sox winning the World Series. This makes the time-travel theory quite a stretch.

Theory #10: It's Man versus Nature

This theory makes a lot of sense. Why? It is both general in scope and also fits the evidence. If the entire plot is simply a play on the enduring struggle of humanity to comprehend and control nature, then there is artistic liberty to communicate this theme on multiple levels, as *Lost* certainly portrays. Spiritual themes, issues of science, human emotions, and how one's past life influences current situations can all be addressed without having all the answers along the way. This would also appear to fit the pattern of *Lost* as it has continued to evolve and change each season, partly on the basis of fan response and collaboration.

Suggestions About the Theories

There are two major kinds of theories on *Lost*. First, there are the overarching views regarding what *Lost* is all about (such as the ten theories just presented). Second, however, are specific theories about what has happened or will happen in specific episodes. For instance, will Walt and Michael return to the island? Is Juliet really on the side of the Others, or not? What will happen to Jin and Sun's baby?

All these theories are an enjoyable part of the *Lost* viewing experience. It's what keeps people tuned in, whether on a casual basis or to the point of watching alertly for appearances of certain numbers along the way. Theories about the world of *Lost*, however, are highly speculative and, so far, have led to little in terms of certainty. Along the way, some theories have become less credible while others remain popular. But ultimately, it's difficult to come to any conclusions regarding these theories. After all, we cannot read the minds of those writing *Lost*. Also, who knows how much of the material in the series has evolved in response to fan theories versus a plan that was in mind from the start? Trying to sort through all this can leave us in the realm of endless speculation, which we discussed in the previous chapter.

That brings us to our final chapter.

Lost Talk

- What are some possible reasons for the fact there are so many theories about *Lost*?

- Do you have a theory that you think makes the most sense of *Lost*?

- What are some of the unanswered questions you still have about *Lost*?

LOST...What to Do About It

*L*ost provides an amazing level of entertainment that has captured the attention of millions of viewers worldwide. And throughout this book, we have looked at a variety of answers to the question, What can be found in *Lost*? In doing so, we have discovered numerous spiritual insights that have relevance to our everyday lives.

We realize it's possible you are reading this book simply because you like *Lost*, and the whole matter of Christianity or following Christ is new or different territory for you. If this sounds like you, we'd like to offer you a L.O.S.T. way to find God:

Look to Jesus

You'll never find God if you look inward. The only way to find spiritual fulfillment is to look beyond yourself to Jesus. He loves you, came to Earth to live, die, and come back to life for you, and offers you a relationship with him today. Jesus said, "I am the way and the truth and the life" (John 14:6). While he is very accepting of all who come to him, you must look to Jesus rather than yourself or any other source as your rescuer and redeemer. His expectation is that you come by faith and not by your good works (Ephesians 2:8-9), and that you accept that Jesus is God's son, who physically came back to life from the dead (1 Corinthians 15:3-11).

Open Your Past to Him

Let's face it. We all sin. The Bible says we have all sinned and fall short of God's glory or standard (Romans 3:23). You may have never considered it this way, but even little sins are enough to keep you from eternity with a perfect God in heaven. The only way any of us can have our sins forgiven, according to the Bible, is through Jesus. His death on the cross paid to cover our wrongs. However, we must ask him for this forgiveness. The apostle John put it this way: "If we confess our sins to God, he can always be trusted to forgive us and take our sins away" (1 John 1:9 cev).

Start with a Prayer of Commitment

There is no magic formula to pray in order to follow Christ, but it is often helpful to have an example to follow. If you would like to begin a relationship with God, the following prayer includes the essential beliefs necessary to take that step:

> God, I ask your son Jesus to enter my life as my leader and rescuer. I know I've messed up and have sinned. Please forgive me. I believe Jesus came back to life from the dead and I place my faith in him for eternal life. I choose to follow Jesus from this moment forward. Please show me how to live for you.

If you just made this request of Jesus, congratulations! Your life will never be the same. You will experience forgiveness, love, joy, and God's peace through life's ups and downs. If you're coming back to begin afresh with Jesus, we want to encourage you in your spiritual journey as well. No matter where you've been, Jesus wants to help you move forward on an adventure of faith in a close relationship with him.

Take Steps to Grow in Christ

Following Christ is a decision—one that brings you into a personal relationship with Jesus every day for the rest of your life. It is the start of a wonderful spiritual journey. We encourage you to tell someone about the decision you have made and to begin the process of growing in your relationship with Christ.

We also invite you to let us know about your decision or your renewed commitment to Christ. Please e-mail lost@johnankerberg.org with your story. We would appreciate the opportunity to share about spiritual growth resources you might find helpful. Please allow us the privilege of enjoying with you your decision to follow Jesus.

If you are already a Christian, we want to know how this resource may have helped your spiritual growth. Please send us your stories and comments to the e-mail address listed above so we can share in how this book has encouraged you. Of course, as *Lost* fans, we also want to see how you are using *Lost* to communicate your faith in Christ to other people. Thanks for sharing these pages with us, and may God bless you as you continue to grow in your relationship with Christ and communicate him to others through your words and actions.

For those who prefer to write via regular mail, please contact us at:

Ankerberg Theological Research Institute
P.O. Box 8977
Chattanooga, TN 37414

Appendix One: Key Characters in *Lost*

WARNING: Contains spoilers! Please do not read the "former main characters" list if you don't want to know what happened to them.

Current Main Characters

Jack Shephard	spinal surgeon/unofficial leader
Kate Austen	fugitive
James "Sawyer" Ford	con man
Sayid Jarrah	former Iraqi military communications officer
Desmond Hume	former Scottish military officer and prisoner, also the sailing racer found in the Swan station hatch
Juliet	fertility doctor; part of the Others
Jin-Soo Kwon	South Korean doorman/assistant to Sun's father
Sun-Hwa Kwon	wife to Jin; homemaker
Benjamin Linus	leader of the Others
Claire Littleton	Australian woman who planned to give up baby for adoption after flight; mother of baby Aaron
John Locke	supervisor for a box company in San Francisco, he helps the survivors by tracking boar (and people) and often provides leadership to the castaways
Paulo	plays golf; unknown background
Nikki	with Paulo; unknown background
Hurley "Hugo" Reyes	lottery winner who worked at Mr. Cluck's Chicken Shack

Former Main Characters

Boone Carlyle	Shannon's half-brother; died from injuries suffered in Beechcraft plane when it fell from a tree in Season One
Ana-Lucia Cortez	former LAPD officer and airport security person; shot by Michael in Season Two
Michael Dawson	left the Others' island in Season Two

Eko	Nigerian drug lord turned priest; killed by smoke monster in Season Three
Libby	psychologist from Los Angeles; shot by Michael in Season Two
Walt Lloyd	Michael's son; left with Michael at end of Season Two
Charlie Pace	musician from the band Driveshaft; former heroine addict
Shannon Rutherford	Boone's half-sister; died in accidental shooting in Season Two

Appendix Two: The Religions of *Lost*

There are many spiritual and religious references in *Lost*, and below is a list of specific characters or events that have made reference to various religious movements.[1] If you are investigating other religions, you will notice that Christianity is the only one that claims its founder, Jesus Christ, came to Earth, lived, died, returned to life, and is alive now. For additional resources on comparative religions and the historical evidence for Jesus and Christianity, check out the materials at the Ankerberg Theological Research Institute at www.johnankerberg.org.

Aboriginal Religion

- The episode "Walkabout" features a spiritual journey (walkabout) Locke planned to take in the Australian outback. Its origin is connected to an aboriginal rite of passage in which young aboriginal men take a six-month journey that includes religious elements.

- The Australian faith healer Isaac of Uluru uses the name "Uluru," which refers to the aboriginal sacred site Ayer's Rock.

Buddhism, Hinduism, and Other Eastern Religions

- Buddhism is featured frequently in *Lost*, including in the very name the Dharma Initiative. The term *dharma* is a Sanskrit word used in Hinduism, Buddhism, and other Eastern faiths that means "the way to higher truths."

- The Dharma Initiative symbol is a bagua, a wheel of destiny from the I Ching often used in feng shui and Taoist geomancy, though usually seen with a central yin/yang to symbolize balance. It is also central to what is in the Destiny Book, which Bai Soo uses to predict love for Jin.

- Reincarnation, mentioned frequently in *Lost*, is taught in many Eastern religious systems.

- "Namaste," spoken at the end of the Dharma orientation video, is a Buddhist greeting with religious overtones.

- The number 108 (a common number in *Lost*) is a highly sacred number to Buddhists, Hindus, and Muslims. There are 108 stars of destiny, 108 beads on a *mala*, 108 seats in the Nepalese parliament, 108 moves in many tai chi sequences, 108 sins in Tibetan Buddhism (that must be overcome to achieve nirvana), and it is the symbol of Siva in Hinduism and of *surat al-Kawthar* in the Qur'an.

- The *dharmacakra*, an eight-spoked wheel of enlightenment in Buddhism, is seen multiple times, including on Isaac's wall and in The *Lost* Experience game.

- An image of a Buddha is on the screen of "brainwashing" images presented to Karl, along with phrases from Eastern philosophy in "Not in Portland."

- A Buddha appears in a painting Desmond sees in a flashback in "Flashes Before Your Eyes."

- In "Not in Portland," Karl saw on a video screen, during a slide show, the statements, "We are causes of our own suffering" and "Think about your life." These likely come from the Four Noble Truths of Buddhism.

- Two Buddhist symbols are seen on the wall of Isaac of Uluru's room in "SOS."

Islam

- Sayid is a practicing Muslim. In "The Greater Good," he goes to a mosque to find Essam, and eventually Essam becomes convinced that a higher calling is bringing them together. Sayid at one point uses Essam's faith to manipulate him into going through with the plan at the center of the CIA sting. After he commits suicide, Sayid feels extremely guilty. The CIA says that his body will be cremated, a practice forbidden by Islam. Sayid's wish is to bring Essam's body to the United States for burial, which results in his tickets being changed to Flight 815.

- In "One of Them," Sayid passes by a wall in Iraq that depicts the Arabic phrase, "Allah, forgive the one who is leaving."

- When Jack wants to burn the dead bodies in the fuselage, Sayid argues with Jack. This is apparently due to Sayid's Islamic belief that cremation is not an acceptable practice.

Judaism and Protestant Christianity

- There is a baby named Aaron. Aaron was the brother of Moses in the biblical book of Exodus.

- Jack is called Moses in "Through the Looking Glass."

- Rose demonstrates aspects of Protestant Christianity through her statements and prayers.

- In "What Kate Did," Mr. Eko tells Locke the story of King Josiah (how the Old Testament law was found). He then shares what he found inside the Bible in the Arrow Station (a splice of film).

- Bibles are found in "Deus ex Machina" (found by Boone near the drug plane) and "The Other 48 Days." In addition, episode titles "Numbers" and "Exodus" are the names of books of the Bible, and one episode was titled "Psalm 23."

- The phrase "the Lord is my shepherd" is likely

the inspiration for Jack's last name, and Christian Shephard is a very Christian-oriented name as well.

- In "House of the Rising Sun," Locke names the skeletons found in the caves Adam and Eve—these two names are found in the biblical book of Genesis.

- The phrase "God loves you as He loved Jacob" appears on the screen during Karl's brainwashing in "Not in Portland."

Kabbalah

- Numerology, an important area of study in Kabbalah, finds extensive usage in *Lost*—especially in relation to the series of numbers used in the hatch.

Paganism and New Age Religions

- A psychic has a premonition and tells Claire she must raise her own child.

- Claire believes in astrology and records her dreams.

- Bernard takes Rose to a faith healer in a remote area of Australia in an attempt to remove her cancer.

- Charlie calls baby Aaron "Turnip Head," a name associated with pagan backgrounds and Samhain/ Halloween.

- Multiple *Lost* characters are found communicating with the dead through dreams or visions (especially Locke).

- Locke builds a sweat lodge as a place of meditation, a practice associated with Native American nature religion.

- Malkin's daughter Charlotte serves as a medium who hears from Eko's brother, Yemi, in a dream.

- The smoke monster (the *Lost*zilla)? No one knows for sure what or who it is, but it certainly could fit one of the monsters of mythology or possibly be an evil spirit or demon.[2]

- Lynn Karnoff is seen reading Tarot cards for Hurley in "Tricia Tanaka Is Dead."

Roman Catholicism

- Charlie was raised Catholic in England.

- Mr. Eko was raised Catholic in Nigeria, but was kidnapped by violent militants in his youth.

- Hurley's mother is very devoutly Catholic, and frequently crosses herself or reminds Hurley that they do not believe in curses.

- Desmond is a fired Catholic monk from Scotland.

- Claire and her baby, Aaron, are baptized in Roman Catholic style in "Fire + Water."

- Locke's mother has a history of psychosis and believes that he was born by immaculate conception, a teaching associated with Mary, mother of Jesus, in Catholic teachings.

Scientology

- At least one writer has suggested that *Lost* is based on Scientology.[3] This is proposed based on Scientology's Buddhist connections, the fact that the Others call themselves the good guys (similar to Scientologists), and that there are similarities between the powers sought by the Others and the powers sought in the teachings of Scientology. However, the religion has never been mentioned in the show to date.

Appendix Three: The Books of *Lost*

Books seen or mentioned on episodes of *Lost* include at least 39 titles in the first three seasons (some fans have found well over 40 if allusions are included). The following list has been adapted from many sources, including Lostpedia.com, Sledgeweb's Lost…Stuff, and Lost Wiki at abc.com.

1. *After All These Years* by Susan Isaacs in "Everybody Hates Hugo"
2. *Alice's Adventures in Wonderland* by Lewis Carroll in "White Rabbit"
3. *Are You There, God? It's Me, Margaret* by Judy Blume in "The Whole Truth"
4. *Bad Twin* by Laurence Shames in "The Long Con" and "Two for the Road"
5. The Bible (see the chapter "*Lost* on the Bible")
6. *A Brief History of Time* by Stephen Hawking in "Not in Portland" and "The Man from Tallahassee"
7. *The Brothers Karamazov* by Fyodor Dostoyevsky in "Maternity Leave"
8. *Carrie* by Stephen King in "A Tale of Two Cities"
9. *Catch-22* by Joseph Heller in "Catch-22"
10. *Dirty Work* by Stuart Woods in "Orientation" and "A Tale of Two Cities"
11. *The Epic of Gilgamesh* in "Collision"
12. *Evil Under the Sun* by Agatha Christie in "Exposé"
13. *The Fountainhead* by Ayn Rand in "Par Avion"
14. *Harry Potter* by J.K. Rowling (general reference) in "Deus Ex Machina"
15. *Heart of Darkness* by Joseph Conrad in "Walkabout" and "Numbers"
16. *Hindsight* by Peter Wright in "Everybody Hates Hugo"
17. I Ching (in the Dharma logos in various episodes)
18. *Island* by Aldous Huxley in "?"
19. *Julius Caesar* by William Shakespeare in "Two for the Road"
20. *Jurassic Park* by Michael Crichton in "Exposé"
21. *Lancelot* by Walker Percy in "Maternity Leave"
22. *Laughter in the Dark* by Vladimir Nabokov in "Flashes Before Your Eyes"

23. *Left Behind* by Jerry Jenkins and Tim LaHaye in the Season Three episode "Left Behind"

24. *Lord of the Flies* by William Golding in "...In Translation" and "What Kate Did"

25. *The Mysterious Island* by Jules Verne in "Whatever the Case May Be"

26. *Occurrence at Owl Creek Bridge* by Ambrose Bierce in "The Long Con"

27. *Of Mice and Men* by John Steinbeck in "Every Man for Himself"

28. *Our Mutual Friend* by Charles Dickens in "Live Together, Die Alone"

29. *Rainbow Six* by Tom Clancy in "Orientation"

30. *Rick Romer's Vision of Astrology* in "Left Behind" (a made-up title for the show)

31. *Stranger in a Strange Land* by Robert Heinlein is the title of the Season Three episode "Stranger in a Strange Land"

32. *A Tale of Two Cities* by Charles Dickens is the title of the Season Three episode "A Tale of Two Cities"

33. *The Third Policeman* by Flann O'Brien in "Man of Science, Man of Faith" and "Orientation"

34. *Through the Looking-Glass* by Lewis Carroll is the title of the Season Three episode "Through the Looking Glass"

35. *To Kill a Mockingbird* by Harper Lee in "The Cost of Living"

36. *The Turn of the Screw* by Henry James in "Orientation"

37. *Watership Down* by Richard Adams in "Confidence Man" and "Left Behind"

38. *The Wizard of Oz* by L. Frank Baum in the title "The Man Behind the Curtain"

39. *A Wrinkle in Time* by Madeleine L'Engle in "Deus Ex Machina"

In addition, four ancient Roman authors are mentioned on the Blast Door Map:

1. Juvenal: Juvenal was a Roman poet and author of *Satires*. He lived during the first to second centuries A.D.

2. Lucan: A first-century A.D. poet who wrote the surviving work *Pharsalia* (meaning "civil war") during the time of Nero, in addition to 13 lost works

that have been named in the writings of others (possibly some interesting *Lost* allusions with the number 13 and civil war).[1]

3. Plautus: An ancient Roman playwright who was born around 254 B.C. There are 20 different written works that remain of his plays.[2]

4. Virgil: A Roman poet from the first century B.C. who authored the *Aeneid* and other poetic works. His relation to *Lost* may be due to his similar usage of religious texts. In the Middle Ages, manuscripts of the *Aeneid* were used in a manner in which a selected text would be chosen at random and interpreted in light of the context of the current situation.[3]

Appendix Four: Character Connections in Seasons One Through Three of *Lost*

During the first three seasons of *Lost*, the myriad cast of characters not only shares experiences on the island, but also includes various connections from their pre-island lives. These connections do not include every activity these characters have shared together; only mirrored flashback actions have been included. The following list provides most of the numerous links between various cast members that continue to influence their lives as island survivors. (Note: This list has been compiled from numerous sources, including the interactive guide at ABC's *Lost* Web site.)

Character	Plus	Connection
Ana-Lucia	Jack	They share a drink before Flight 815. She also works with Jack's dad.
	Sawyer	Runs into him outside of an Australian bar while with Christian Shephard, Jack's father.
Boone	Sawyer	Run into one another in an Australian police station in "Hearts & Minds."
	Shannon	Stepbrother and sister, who share a complex past.
Charlie	Desmond	Desmond spots Charlie playing guitar on the street after his breakup with Penelope.
	Hurley	Shared the same hotel the night before their flight. Hurley also mocks Charlie's band, Driveshaft, when finding their CD in a local store.
	Locke	Big fan of the band Driveshaft and owns both of their albums.
Desmond	Charlie	Desmond spots Charlie playing street guitar in "Flashes Before Your Eyes."
	Jack	Both are shown running stairs in "Man of Science, Man of Faith."
	Libby	Libby gives Desmond his boat in "Live Together, Die Alone."

	Sayid	Both know Imam, as revealed in "One of Them."
Eko	Claire	Claire's psychic is the father of the young girl Eko is sent to visit in "?"
	Libby	Libby enters a conversation Eko is having at the airport in "?"
Ethan	Juliet	Says hello to Juliet in a hallway in "Not in Portland."
Hurley (Hugo)	Artz	Hurley cuts in front of Artz at the airport in "Exodus."
	Charlie	Stayed in the same hotel before Flight 815. Hurley also mocks Charlie's Driveshaft CD in "Everybody Hates Hugo."
	Jin	Hurley is on Korean television in the background when Jin visits the environmental secretary in "…In Translation."
	Libby	Fellow mental institute patient in "Dave."
	Locke	Hurley's former boss is Locke's box company boss.
	Walt	Walt's Spanish comic book is revealed to be Hugo's in "Exodus, Part 2."
Jack	Ana-Lucia	Meet in the airport bar in "Exodus, Part 1."
	Clair	We discover they are half siblings in "Par Avion."
	Desmond	Both are seen running stairs in "Man of Science, Man of Faith."
	Jin	Jin waits behind Jack in the airport line in "White Rabbit."
	Shannon	Jack sees her dad in the hospital in two episodes.
Jin	Hurley	Hurley is on Korean television in the background when Jin visits the environmental secretary in "…In Translation."
	Jack	Jin waits behind Jack in the airport line in "White Rabbit."
	Sayid	Jin passes Sayid on the way to the restroom in "Exodus, Part 2."
Kate	Sayid	Sayid is on the TV news behind Kate in "What Kate Did." Kate's dad also shows Sayid Kate's picture in "One of Them."

	Sawyer	Share a common friend, Cassidy, in "Left Behind." He is also served at a diner by Kate's mom in "The Long Con."
Libby	Desmond	Libby gives Desmond his boat in "Live Together, Die Alone."
	Eko	Libby enters a conversation Eko is having at the airport in "?"
	Hurley	Fellow mental institute patient in "Dave."
Locke	Charlie	Big fan of the band Driveshaft and owns both of their albums.
	Hurley	Hurley's former boss is Locke's box company boss.
	Michael	Locke rolls by Michael in his wheelchair at the airport in "Exodus, Part 2."
	Rose	Locke picks up Rose's pills for her in "SOS."
	Sayid	John is the home inspector for Sayid's Nadia in "Solitary."
Michael	Locke	Locke rolls by Michael in his wheelchair at the airport in "Exodus, Part 2."
	Walt	Michael's son.
Rose	Locke	Locke picks up Rose's pills for her in "SOS."
Sawyer	Ana-Lucia	Ana runs into Sawyer outside of an Australian bar while with Christian Shephard, Jack's father.
	Boone	They run into one another in an Australian police station in "Hearts & Minds."
	Kate	Share a common friend, Cassidy, in "Left Behind." He is also served at a diner by Kate's mom in "The Long Con."
Sayid	Desmond	Both know Imam, as revealed in "One of Them."
	Jin	Jin passes Sayid on the way to the restroom in "Exodus, Part 2."
	Kate	Sayid is in the TV news behind Kate in "What Kate Did." Kate's dad also shows Sayid Kate's picture in "One of Them."
	Locke	John is the home inspector for Sayid's Nadia in "Solitary."

	Shannon	Shannon has issues with Sayid's luggage in "Exodus, Part 1."
Shannon	Boone	Stepbrother and sister who share a complex past.
	Jack	Jack sees Shannon's dad in the hospital in two episodes.
	Sayid	Shannon has issues with Sayid's luggage in "Exodus, Part 1."
Sun	Jin	Run into each other in "House of the Rising Sun" and are later married under awkward circumstances.
Walt	Michael	Father and son with a difficult past.
	Hurley	Walt reads his Spanish comic book after the crash.

Acknowledgments

We are thankful for the many individuals who have contributed to the research and spiritual insights found in this book. Though there are two names on the cover, many have contributed to the thoughts shared in these pages.

John:

Thanks to...

Bob Hawkins, Terry Glaspey, Steve Miller, LaRae Weikert, and the team at Harvest House for their vision, partnership, and excellent editing throughout the various stages of this project.

The team at ATRI—Darlene, Michelle, Alan, Beth, Ben, Marlene, Steve, and Jack—thank you for your additions to the spiritual insights along the way. This job was truly a team effort!

Dillon:

Thanks to...

Deborah, Ben, and Natalie—you are the most priceless treasures in my life. Thanks for understanding when I had to spend times writing and for being the ones who bring my life the most joy.

My friends and family—this books exists because of your generous prayers, relationships, and support. I especially want to thank my mom, Tiffany, and Travis for sticking with me through the ups and downs of life. I love you all!

To my friend Mark Tobey—thanks for giving me my start in publishing. May God continue to bless your efforts.

To the *Lost* cast, crew, and production team—thanks for a great show that explores the depths of humanity and spirituality with the utmost quality.

To the numerous contributors of *Lost* research around the world—this book would not have been possible without your collaboration. A special thanks to Losthatch.com for their keyword searchable transcripts, to Lostpedia.com for your thorough details, and to Sledgeweb's *Lost* Web site for insightful special investigations on *Lost*.

Ultimately, thanks to Jesus Christ for the opportunity to serve others through writing.

Notes

Opening Page

1. Cited in Lynette Porter and David Lowery, *Unlocking the Meaning of* Lost (Naperville, IL: Sourcebooks, 2007), p. 239.

Why Should I Read This Book?

1. Paul R. La Monica, "For ABC, DVR Viewers Don't Get 'Lost,'" *Media Biz*, May 7, 2007. Accessed at http://mediabiz.blogs.cnnmoney .com/2007/05/07/for-abc-dvr-viewers-dont-get-lost/.

2. "Lost (TV Series)" at http://en.wikipedia.org/wiki/Lost_(TV_series)#Cast_and_characters.

3. Ibid.

4. Tim Ryan, "High filming costs force ABC network executives to consider relocating," *Honolulu Star-Bulletin*, January 26, 2005. Accessed at http://starbulletin.com/2005/01/26/news/story2.html.

Chapter 1—*Lost* on God

1. Lynnette Porter and David Lavery, *Unlocking the Meaning of* Lost (Naperville, IL: Sourcebooks, 2007), p. 140.

2. See John Ankerberg and Dillon Burroughs, *What's the Big Deal About Jesus?* (Eugene, OR: Harvest House, 2007).

3. N.T. Wright in an interview on "A Response to ABC's the Search for Jesus," on *The John Ankerberg Show*, 2001.

Chapter 2—*Lost* on Prayer

1. "Faith Commitment," by the Barna Group. Accessed at http://www .barna.org/FlexPage.aspx?Page=Topic&TopicID=19.

2. From www.dictionary.com.

3. From http://www.quotegarden.com/prayer.html.

Chapter 4—*Lost* on Miracles

1. Gary Habermas, "Jesus: The Search Continues," *The John Ankerberg Show*, 2002.

2. William Lane Craig, "Jesus: The Search Continues."

3. "Some Well-Known Miracles of Jesus," Bible Resource Center. Accessed online at http://www.bibleresourcecenter.org/vsItemDisplay .dsp&objectID=F38BB037-BFF6-47FE-A828BEA35B562AE8&method =display.

Chapter 5—*Lost* on Trust and Secrets

1. Thanks to Sledgeweb's Lost Stuff site for these observations at http://lost .cubit.net/themesView.php?id=450.

2. See http://lostpedia.com/wiki/Deceptions_and_cons.

Chapter 6—*Lost* on Good and Evil

1. For these and additional uses of black and white in *Lost*, see http://www .hanttula.com/projects/lost/other-notes/references-to-black-white.

2. Erwin Lutzer, *Where Was God? Answers to Tough Questions About God and Natural Disasters* (Wheaton, IL: Tyndale, 2006), p. 6.

3. C.S. Lewis, *Mere Christianity*, chapter one, as quoted at http://yourdaily cslewis.blogspot.com/.

Chapter 7—*Lost* on the Bible

1. See http://www.lostpedia.com/wiki/Jesus_Stick.

2. Ibid.

3. Ibid.

4. See the freeze-frame photos at http://lost.cubit.net/forum/index.php? action=gallery;sa=view;id=250.

5. Eric Van Lustbader, Robert Ludlum's *The Bourne Betrayal* (New York: Warner Books, 2007), pp. 348-49.

6. Adapted from Vincent McCann, "Are All Religions More or Less the Same?" Spotlight Ministries, 2000. Accessed at http://www.spotlight ministries.org.uk/plural.htm.

Chapter 8—*Lost* on Dreams and Visions

1. As cited at http://lostpedia.com/wiki/Newspaper_clipping.

2. Or 18, if Pharaoh's dream is counted as two dreams.

3. George Sweeting, *Today in the Word* (Chicago, IL: Moody Publishing, 1989), p. 40. Cited at http://www.bible.org/illus.asp?topic_id=1190.

Chapter 9—*Lost* on Leadership

1. J. Oswald Sanders, *Spiritual Leadership* (Chicago, IL: Moody Press, 1994), p. 22.

2. Neil S. Wilson, ed., *The Handbook of Bible Application* (Wheaton, IL: Tyndale House Publishers, 1992), p. 379.

Chapter 10—*Lost* on Numbers

1. From http://www.lostpedia.com/wiki/The_Numbers.

2. For further details, see http://en.wikipedia.org/wiki/Lost_%28season_4%29#Fandom_and_popular_culture.

3. See http://www.cafepress.com/4815162342.com.

4. Adapted from the list at http://www.lostpedia.com/wiki/The_Numbers.

5. Ibid.

6. For the full list, see http://www.4815162342.com/forum/viewtopic.php?t=4748.

7. A special thanks to Mike Hanttula's "Lost Notebook" for this adapted information at http://www.hanttula.com/projects/lost/other-notes/repetition-of-names.

8. Ibid.

Chapter 11—*Lost* on Redemption

1. Jeff Jenson, "The Beach Boys," *Entertainment Weekly*, April 15, 2005, p. 22.

2. Lynette Porter and David Lowery, *Unlocking the Meaning of Lost: An Unauthorized Guide* (Naperville, IL: Sourcebooks, 2007), p. 218.

Chapter 12—*Lost* on Death

1. For a complete list of these deaths, see http://www.losthatch.com/characters.aspx.

2. C.S. Lewis, cited from http://www.quotationspage.com/quote/37807.html.

Chapter 13—*Lost* on the Afterlife

1. See "Thematic Motifs," *Lost* TV series. Accessed at http://en.wikipedia.org/wiki/Lost_%28TV_series%29#Mythology. Further details on the connections of philosophers in *Lost* can be accessed at http://lostpedia.com/wiki/Philosophy.

Chapter 14—Researching the World of *Lost*

1. See the complete list at http://www.lost-media.com/modules.php?name=News&file=article&sid=2589&mode=thread&order=0&thold=0.

2. Ibid, p. 257.

3. From http://www.lostpedia.com/wiki/The_Lost_Experience.

4. Ibid.

5. Ibid., pp. 254-55.

6. Paul R. La Monica, "For ABC, DVR Viewers Don't Get 'Lost,'" *Media Biz*, May 7, 2007. Accessed at http://mediabiz.blogs.cnnmoney.com/2007/05/07/for-abc-dvr-viewers-dont-get-lost/.

7. The following statistics are all based on research on these sites as of July 2007.

8. See the timeline at http://lostpedia.com/wiki/Timeline:December_2004.

9. See http://www.lostpedia.com/wiki/Time/Theories.

10. For the reverse audio theories about Walt, see http://lost.cubit.net/forum/index.php?action=gallery;cat=1.

Chapter 15—Researching the (Many) Theories of *Lost*

1. See http://lostwiki.abc.com/page/Purgatory.

Appendix Two: The Religions of *Lost*

1. A special thanks to Sledgeweb's Lost Stuff for several of the connections that appear in this appendix. Accessed at http://lost.cubit.net.

2. See an excellent parallel in the Mortician god Cynothoglys at http://ante diluvia.pbwiki.com/Cynothoglys.

3. See "Lost is Scientology" at http://lostwiki.abc.com/page/Scientology.

Appendix Three: The Books of *Lost*

1. An English translation of Lucan's writing is available online at http://www.gutenberg.org/browse/authors/l#a316.

2. English translations of many of Plautus's writings are available at http://www.gutenberg.org/browse/authors/p#a2406.

3. For more on this, see http://en.wikipedia.org/wiki/Virgil#Mysticism_and_hidden_meanings.

About the Authors

John Ankerberg, host of the award-winning *John Ankerberg Show*, has three earned degrees: a Master of Arts in church history and the philosophy of Christian thought, a Master of Divinity from Trinity International University, and a Doctor of Ministry from Luther Rice Seminary. With Dr. John Weldon, he has coauthored *What Do Mormons Really Believe?*, *Fast Facts on Islam*, the Facts On... series of apologetic booklets, and other volumes.

Dillon Burroughs, a full-time writer who has worked with a number of bestselling authors, is a graduate of Dallas Theological Seminary, coauthor of *What's the Big Deal About Jesus?* with John Ankerberg, a member of the Society for the Study of *Lost* (loststudies.com), and a contributor to Lostpedia.com. He lives with his wife, Deborah, and two children in Tennessee.